How God Grows
a
Woman
of Prayer

A Devotional
Journal

ANITA HIGMAN
& MARIAN LESLIE

BARBOUR BOOKS
An Imprint of Barbour Publishing, Inc.

Published by Barbour Books, an imprint of Barbour Publishing, Inc., P.O. Box 719, Uhrichsville, Ohio 44683, www.barbourbooks.com

Our mission is to publish and distribute inspirational products offering exceptional value and biblical encouragement to the masses.

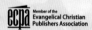
Member of the
Evangelical Christian
Publishers Association

Printed in China.

"More things are
wrought by prayer
than this world
dreams of."

ALFRED, LORD TENNYSON

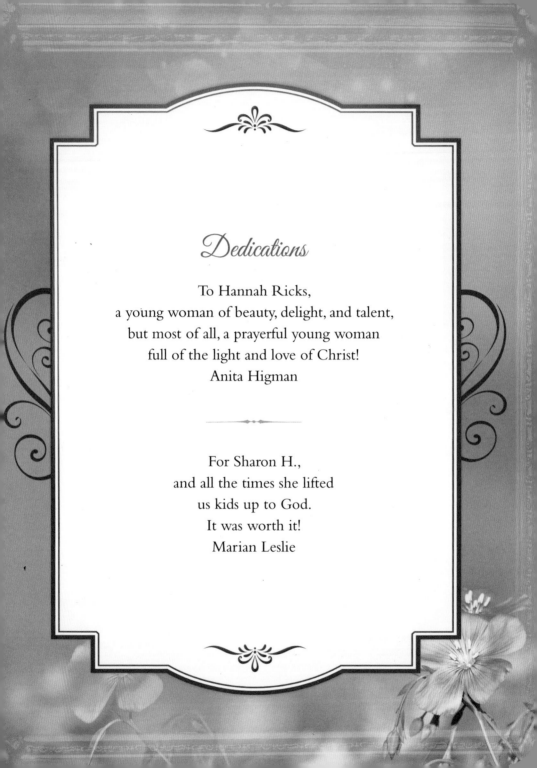

Dedications

To Hannah Ricks,
a young woman of beauty, delight, and talent,
but most of all, a prayerful young woman
full of the light and love of Christ!
Anita Higman

For Sharon H.,
and all the times she lifted
us kids up to God.
It was worth it!
Marian Leslie

Introduction

———————◆———————

When you talk to God, do you expect a miracle? The fact that we, as fallen creatures, can always expect an answer to our prayers from the God of the universe—whether it be a "yes" or "no" or a "wait"—is a miracle in itself. Prayer is a supernatural communication with the Creator of all things, but it is also a profoundly intimate exchange.

We are assured in God's Word that He loves us with a passionate earnestness, an attentive love that we cannot fathom, and yet we seem determined to follow our own path no matter how dangerous or deadly. It is often in the darkest places that we long for the arms of the One who loves us, who made us. No matter where we are, in prayer, our hearts run home to God. Where they belong.

Shall we begin that journey with God—that intimate journey called prayer?

A Bit of a Toad

A good friendship takes time, effort, and sensitivity, but a healthy friendship is not one sided. For instance, how would you feel if you had a friend—let's call her Amelia—who only comes around when she wants to borrow something—like your fondue pot, your designer sunglasses, or your car with a full tank of gas? Amelia asks, "Could you babysit while I get the polish freshened on my toenails? Oh, and I need to unload big-time since my boss has become this miserly, manipulative, and mean-spirited mule of a man. Oh, and would you minding helping me with my daughter's costume for the school's talent show? This year she's a singing toad."

These might not be outrageous things to ask of a buddy, and yet if that's all Amelia ever came calling for, wouldn't you think your friend was a bit of a toad, too? Why? Because you want a relationship in which someone not only needs you, but loves you. Wouldn't you think that Amelia's brand of friendship wasn't intimate, wasn't real?

Christ would like to be our friend—a real one. And if we only go to Him in prayer, begging for a better job, better health, and a bigger house, might we not be sending the same message, that we're more interested in the "getting" than the loving?

Lord, please help me love You as a real friend and not just for what You can give me. Amen.—AH

One Word That Changes Everything

He was despised and rejected by mankind, a man of suffering, and familiar with pain. Like one from whom people hide their faces he was despised, and we held him in low esteem.
ISAIAH 53:3

Have you ever felt abandoned? Misplaced? Abused? Rejected? Forgotten? We have all felt those feelings from time to time. What can we do about them? Well, the world has plenty of answers. Mask the anguish with painkillers, addictions, false teachings under the guise of spiritual enlightenment, and myriad other bogus remedies. You name it; the world is selling it as an alternative like the man hollering on the street corner selling snake oil. One soon discovers, though, that the world's answers are as real as the tooth fairy. Their cures will only make one feel more forlorn, emptier, and more forgotten than ever.

What to do? Face the unhappy pangs of this life by holding the hand of the One who has known all these trials—the One who knows better than anyone on earth what it feels like to suffer, to be rejected, abused, and forgotten. So, how does one do that, exactly? With the one word that the enemy of our souls wants us to forget. One word that can change everything—can bring meaning and hope, and make that misery and aloneness flee to hell where it belongs.

It's prayer.

Father, help me to turn to You alone for
my comfort instead of the world. Amen.—AH

Imagine This. . . .

*And all are justified freely by his grace through
the redemption that came by Christ Jesus.*
ROMANS 3:24

Imagine this. What if a stranger came up to you on the street and handed you a pearl necklace. Then after smiling, the man walked away? What would you do? Try to give the necklace back? Would you think it was stolen, or maybe that it was no more than a plastic bauble?

Yet what if you had it appraised and it was a genuine pearl necklace and valuable—in fact, a priceless treasure? You might then fret that the man would return and expect something from you—that you'd have to work to truly own such a costly gift. Or would you then think that the man was loony for offering such a precious gift to a mere stranger?

You get the drift. That is what Christ has done for us with His gift of life eternal—with His costly sacrifice on the cross. Still we treat Him like the man on the street, thinking He must be either phony or foolish, or that if He is real, there are strings attached to His good and perfect gift.

Okay, so what if we do finally understand this free gift of grace? What do we do with it? Accept it. Rejoice over it. Maybe even shout. Then thank Him—in that wonderful communication called prayer.

---

*Jesus, I want to be daily reminded of the pricelessness of Your gift of grace.
Thank You for all you have done and continue to do. Amen.—AH*

That Little Inner Mechanism

"Do not let your hearts be troubled.
You believe in God; believe also in me."
JOHN 14:1

There is something wonderful about a music box—that treasure chest of sweet and melodic tranquility—and if one believed in enchantment, it might be called the music of fairies. What if that music box were wound up over and over and over without ever letting it wind back down again? What if the little winding key got tighter and tighter until the inner mechanisms—like the cylinder, the comb, and the flywheel— could no longer work? It would no longer be able to play its beautiful music.

Well, when our hearts become troubled with the cares of this world, we can no longer play the music we were created to play. We are essentially broken. So, how does one undo, unravel, and slow down when our own winding key has been wound too tightly and our inner mechanism—our soul—can no longer function properly? We should take all our troubles to the Lord in prayer. Every heartache. Every disappointment. Every sorrow. He will let us rest in Him, and disentangle ourselves from the human stresses, so that we can rise again. So that we can once again, play our music to a world that needs to hear it.

Lord, when I am feeling anxious, help me to remember that
You hold me in the palm of Your hand. You have the power
to restore and refresh my weary soul. Amen.—AH

Tumbling the Stones

But just as he who called you is holy,
so be holy in all you do.
1 Peter 1:15–16

If you've ever spent time beachcombing, you know that the stones that get trapped in between the big rocks often get tossed and whirled a great deal. So much so, that the edges get worked off, making them the smoothest of all. The colors and nuances and unique markings are accentuated. In other words, their beauty is brought out by the process of the constant stirring and abrasion—rock tumbling against rock. When you pick them up and roll them around in your palm they feel like the shell of an egg. It's those stones that become part of your trove of little beach treasures.

God uses the tumbling turbulence of our lives to work off our edges—those jagged, sinful, rebellious edges that keep us from being all that we were meant to be.

Being tumbled can be painful—stone hitting stone can't be all that fun—but the outcome will be holiness and a loveliness of spirit. We will be treasures, brighter than diamonds and more precious than gold.

Pray that God can use your tumbling trials to bring out the beauty of your soul.

Dear Lord, please use the turbulent times of my life to help make me beautiful in my spirit, so that I can glorify You and be all that You created me to be.—AH

When Our Hearts Are Captured

Then you and the Levites and the foreigners residing among you shall rejoice in all the good things the LORD your God has given to you and your household.
DEUTERONOMY 26:11

How does a person react when standing at the mouth of the Grand Canyon—when taking in the majestic spires and gorges that are awash in radiant color? What can a mother do when she holds her newborn baby for the first cuddling and cooing moments after birth—and when the infant grasps her hand as if to say, "I know you!" How can we express delight when we stand under a fig tree eating a piece of luscious fruit so ripe and juicy that it makes our taste buds do the tango? Or when our hearts are captured by a soul-aching melody or verse of poetry or the first glowing sparks of true love?

Our hearts long to thank someone, and it would only be natural to praise the giver of such gifts. Praise is prayer in one of its most beautiful forms. A grateful heart can more easily crowd out anger and envy, pride and strife. It can break open the most hardened heart to let in the light and splendor of heaven.

So, shall we raise our hands? Shall we create a hallelujah moment? Shall we rejoice in all the good things that the Lord our God has given us? We shall!

Father, thank You for all the beauty, joy, and splendor that life has to offer. Please cultivate in me a grateful spirit. Amen.—AH

The Radiance of His Splendor

In the year that King Uzziah died, I saw the Lord, high and exalted, seated on a throne; and the train of his robe filled the temple. Above him were seraphim, each with six wings: With two wings they covered their faces, with two they covered their feet, and with two they were flying.

ISAIAH 6:1–2

Society has used the words *awesome* and *incredible* and *glorious* so loosely for so long that the words no longer fill us with pause or wonder. Perhaps we mentally shrug when we hear those words batted about in conversation. People might say they had an incredible trip or they bought some awesome stilettoes or they had a glorious day at the spa. In spite of this misapplication of these expressions, there are things that do fulfill the authentic meaning of these words.

The book of Isaiah tells us that the Lord is exalted, seated on a throne, and the train of His robe fills the temple. Isaiah also talks about the angels who attend Him and worship Him—that their wings cover their faces—surely because of the radiance of His splendor. How fearsome and humbling and magnificent that sight must be!

In fact, this holy scene in the heavenlies should remind us that one day every knee shall bow and every tongue confess that He is Lord. Why wait until that final day? Why not give praise to the One—the only One—who is worthy of our raised hearts and hands? The One who is truly incredible and awesome and glorious!

Lord God, help me to comprehend Your magnitude and glory. I want to be awestruck by You. Amen.—AH

This Cobblestone Journey

When Americans travel to Europe they will see that the streets of some of the more ancient cities are lined with charming paths of cobblestone. But the romance of these quaint streets and laneways stop cold when you trip and fall on the uneven stones. Yes, you will flail around. You will let out a shriek. Horror will flash across your face, but no one can reach you in time. You're on your own.

Then you hit the hard, unforgiving rock with brute force. There might be a bloody nose, a fractured cheekbone, a broken kneecap as well as some painful scratches covering your palms. So, that merry strolling moment of joy has turned ugly. Suddenly that old-world look has as much charm as a French pastry lying in the Dumpster.

Sounds a bit like life, doesn't it?

There is most excellent news, though. God's Word says that even though there will be trouble on life's path, He has overcome this world. Even when we tumble and cut ourselves on the sharp stones of life, it is comforting to know that He will not only mend our wounds in the here and now, but through the acceptance of His offer of redemption, He will someday take us away from this fallen world to a place that knows no pain, no trouble, no joy turned ugly. So, take heart, friends. He has overcome the world. Let's remember to thank Him daily!

Jesus, I have nothing to fear because You have prepared a way for me. I choose to trust in You. Amen.—AH

The Most Beautiful Words

So God created mankind in his own image, in the image of God
he created them; male and female he created them.
GENESIS 1:27

Flowers—bluebonnets, Mexican primrose, and Indian paintbrush—
picked in delight on a spring day are sometimes pressed inside the pages
of a book. When time passes, and one revisits the flowers, they are dried
and flat and lifeless, mere shadows of what they were. The vibrant colors
are gone, the perfume no longer enchants, and the wonder of their
beauty is only a distant memory. Yet there lingers an endearing essence
of what once was. . . .

That is so much like humans in their fallen state.

We were made in the image of God, but because of sin, we became
shriveled and faded. Yet with the sacrifice Jesus made for us with His
very life, mankind has hope to return to the beauty that once was ours.
When those who belong to Christ die and pass into eternity they will
be given glorified bodies renewed with life and color. Not for a short
time like the flowers of the field, but for all eternity.

If you've never asked the Lord to be yours, to acknowledge your sin
and take Him into your heart—well, what has been stopping you? They
will be the most beautiful words you will ever speak and the most life-
changing prayer you will ever pray. . . .

God, restore, refresh, and reconcile me to Yourself. Help me to become
all You have created me to be. Amen.—AH

As Easy as Breathing

Pray continually.
1 Thessalonians 5:17

Praying continually? Don't those two words in the Bible seem a bit foreign to us? In fact, the words stand alone—looking rather stark. We stare at them, wondering how anyone, no matter how holy, could accomplish such a command. There would be no time left for working or playing or eating or resting.

Perhaps the scripture means that to pray without ceasing is when we are in natural conversation with Him during the day—as if we were chatting with a friend on and off while taking a long pleasant walk together.

For instance, you might thank God when you wake up to a new morning. You might ask Him to bless your breakfast and invite Him to guide you through the day. You might feel compelled to breathe a prayer of thanksgiving when you have a near miss with another car on your way to work. Perhaps you'd want to praise Him for the project you successfully completed, and then request that He help your boss who's having a bad day or heal a coworker who's having some health issues. This kind of day does reflect the 1 Thessalonians scripture—that is, to stay so close to God that one finds praying as easy and comfortable as breathing.

Father, please be present in my heart and thoughts always. Never let our communion and fellowship be severed. I want every area of my life to be committed to You through sincere, continual prayer. Amen.—AH

Seen by Others

"And when you pray, do not be like the hypocrites, for they love to pray standing in the synagogues and on the street corners to be seen by others. Truly I tell you, they have received their reward in full. But when you pray, go into your room, close the door and pray to your Father, who is unseen."
MATTHEW 6:5–6

Have you ever heard a beautiful prayer in a large cathedral, and the words echoed and sang with a stirring rhythm and spiritual uplift of its own? Some people are gifted at praying in public. They know how to move and excite their audiences with an eloquent presentation. Unfortunately, humans have to be careful not to enjoy the admiration of the crowd too much, since it would be easy to forget to whom the prayers are intended and begin to seek the approval of man over God.

Jesus encourages us in the book of Matthew to have a humble attitude when it comes to prayer by finding a quiet place to talk to Him, away from the attentive crowds. Does that mean we cannot pray in public? No, but it would be wise to be watchful of our motives, since a heartfelt closet prayer would surely be more welcome than a prayer that is raised up to impress the masses.

Where is your favorite quiet place to talk to God?

Lord, give me a spirit of humility and sincerity when I pray in front of others. Help me to remember that prayer should not be used to show others how godly and well spoken I am, but to connect with You, the living God. Amen.—AH

Why Fasting?

"But when you fast, put oil on your head and wash your face, so that it will not be obvious to others that you are fasting, but only to your Father, who is unseen; and your Father, who sees what is done in secret, will reward you."
MATTHEW 6:17–18

Eating has become a sport in our country, a mania—perhaps even a god. So, to commit to giving up a meal or two occasionally or giving up solid food for a little while in order to spend more time with the Lord seems impossible.

It isn't.

What is the purpose of fasting? First of all, planning meals, buying food, cooking, and cleaning up is time consuming, and when we give it up even for a day, it allows us more time to turn our hearts toward heaven. Second, fasting, along with our prayer, can be powerful as we hear the Lord more clearly, sense His presence more keenly, and see the work of the Holy Spirit moving in our lives. Fasting can give us a new perspective, one that is more God centered, peace filled, refreshing, freeing, healing, and life changing.

If you have health issues that keep you from traditional fasting, you might try fasting TV shows or desserts. If you do fast and pray, the Gospel of Matthew says not to grandstand about it but to do it quietly, and then God will reward you.

Father, give me the desire and the discipline to seek You in prayer in a more devoted and focused way. Amen.—AH

One Soul at a Time

"If my people, who are called by my name, will humble themselves and pray and seek my face and turn from their wicked ways, then I will hear from heaven, and I will forgive their sin and will heal their land."
2 Chronicles 7:14

If you have the courage to watch the evening news you know that we live in perilous times. We also live in wicked times. People don't seem to care anymore about watching out for their neighbors. About lying and cheating a bit here and there. About living together first to see if that marriage thing might be for them. About honoring the sanctity of life and family and worship and God. In fact, the word *sin* has gone out of vogue, but just because a nation hides its transgressions doesn't mean people are getting away with them. Sound familiar? Just as Adam and Eve hid in the garden after they sinned, we as a nation are trying to hide our shame.

What can we do? It starts with one soul at a time. If we will humble ourselves and pray and seek His face and turn from our wicked ways, then He will hear us, forgive us, and heal our land. Let this be our personal petition, our greatest ambition, and our heart prayer as a nation.

Lord, You have the power to guide and restore nations. Please help the people of this country to acknowledge their sin and their need for You. Amen.—AH

A Sacramental Ointment

Is anyone among you sick? Let them call the elders of the church to pray over them and anoint them with oil in the name of the Lord.
JAMES 5:14

Sometimes when we think of the Bible, we think of such ancient people and cultures that the Holy Scriptures feel as close and accessible and understandable as a distant planet. Yet God has never changed. He is the same in our modern world as He was in ancient times. Even though the idea of an ill person being prayed over and anointed with oil by the elders of the church seems too archaic of a tradition to be considered today, think again.

In Bible times, people used oil for various reasons—both medicinal and spiritual. One purpose was to use oil like a sacramental ointment poured on someone's head as that person was prayed over for healing. There is, of course, no supernatural power in the oil itself, but God has the authority to use this act of obedience, this symbolic oil, as a way to heal.

So, when illness comes to you or your family in mind, body, or spirit, consider this scripture and know there is significance in the biblical traditions, even today.

God, thank You for hearing my prayers—whether they are quickly whispered or accompanied with oil. Help me to better understand and appreciate the traditions You have put in place for Your followers. Amen.—AH

That Volatile Liquid

"Therefore I tell you, do not worry about your life, what you will eat or drink;
or about your body, what you will wear. Is not life more than food, and the body
more than clothes? Look at the birds of the air; they do not sow or reap
or store away in barns, and yet your heavenly Father feeds them.
Are you not much more valuable than they?"
MATTHEW 6:25–26

Women tend to be like vats of worry. We toss everything imaginable into that emotional messy brew. You know what I mean—the many frets that we distill down when we choose to hand-wring through our days and toss and turn through our nights. Then we pour that volatile liquid into spray bottles, and we hose down our friends and family with it. Yeah, we're not talking about spritzing them with the calming and cooling lavender water that comes from a heart full of faith in the One who holds us in the palm of His mighty hand. We're talking about the muggy and malodorous perspiration from a life drenched in fear. Oy!

Jesus asks us if we can add a single hour to our life with worry. We cannot. Jesus also says that the birds are cared for, and that we are much more valuable to Him. So, what are we to do?

We can pray.

It's real. It's powerful. And our friends and family will thank us!

Father, remind me that You're in control.
I place my burdens and fears in Your capable hands. Amen.—AH

Almost Too Much to Hope For

Husbands, love your wives,
just as Christ loved the church and gave himself up for her.
EPHESIANS 5:25

Everybody loves a wedding. Why? Well, beyond the scrumptious food, the enchanting attire, and the glorious setting—the idea of a man and woman, speaking words of tender affection, so deeply in love and so attentive to each other's joy and delight, is contagious, intoxicating, and unabashedly beautiful.

To think that is the way Christ loves us is almost too much to take in. It is almost too much to hope for.

Yet it is the truth.

Christ loves us intimately and passionately, not romantically as in human terms, but with a steadfast care and devotion that is beyond our human understanding. His love is forever. Imagine the God of the universe with such perfect love. For You. For me. Who can resist that kind of sweet affection? Who among you really wants to turn your back on this exquisite overture of love? It is contagious, intoxicating, and unabashedly beautiful!

So then, reach your heart to heaven.

Embrace His love.

The Lord is waiting for your prayerful answer, and He is hoping it will be yes!

God, the depth of Your love is unfathomable. I want to be
swept up in it and transformed by it. Amen.—AH

Where We Belong

Jesus, knowing that they intended to come and make him king by force, withdrew again to a mountain by himself.
JOHN 6:15

When Jesus came, people saw Him in a hundred different ways, and what they wanted from Him wasn't always salvation. They sought political power. They wanted freedom, not always from their fallen state, but from their enemies. They wanted a king who could be their champion, their leader, their conqueror for all their causes.

But Jesus? Well, He was much more concerned about their hearts and prayers than the power He could wield. Jesus didn't come to overthrow empires, but to overthrow sin and death. Not to fight against political enemies, but the enemy (Satan) of our souls.

Jesus is a king, yes. In fact, He is the King of kings and Lord of lords. He will indeed reign forever and ever. While on earth, He said, "Follow Me." He was the Good Shepherd, and He came with a staff, not a sword. He wanted to lead us not into a worldly battle, but away from hell. Away from all that is unholy. Toward the home where we belong.

So, when Christ says, "Follow Me," what do you do? Where is your heart? What is in your prayer?

Jesus, help me to follow You with boldness, joy, and trust. I want to see life through heaven-bound eyes. Be my everything. Amen.—AH

A Daily Jolt for the Spirit

In all your ways submit to him,
and he will make your paths straight.
PROVERBS 3:6

Have you ever been caught in a rut for so long that it started to feel like a hopeless abyss? That is just where the enemy of your soul wants you to be—unable to be effective in this hurting and needy world, unable to share the love of Christ, unable to reflect His glorious light.

So, how does one emerge from those endless furrows that represent the monotone, monochrome, grind of the everyday—the looking down into the mire instead of gazing up into the splendor? Just like the vehicle stuck in the rut, sometimes we need a jolt to pull us out. Prayer is that daily jolt for our spirit. Prayer is what gets us back on track, headed where we need to go.

If we submit to God in prayer, He will guide us on this earthly road. He will help us stay out of that dreaded rut and free of the daily abyss of hopelessness, so that we might rise up and be all that Christ wants us to be in a world that needs His love.

That is a promise we can take to our knees every day.

Holy Spirit, don't ever let me lose hope. You are my protector, provider,
and comforter. Even when I feel desperately alone and downtrodden,
help me to remember that You are always there for me. Amen.—AH

When Life Hands You Lemons

*And we know that in all things God works for the good of those
who love him, who have been called according to his purpose.*
Romans 8:28

Your boss recommends a new hire for a promotion—the same position you'd been working toward for ten years. Your best friend betrays your trust in a way that makes you question all your relationships. A long-needed and much-anticipated vacation must be canceled because of illness. What is this?

It's called life.

You've heard the old saying that you should make lemonade out of the lemons that life hands you, and yet you wonder, *Where is the sugar? The chipped ice? The crystal pitcher to put it all in?*

And then you realize that the world expects you to provide all the extras with your own personal ingenuity and grit. Yet the steam that comes from our own strength will soon run out. We humans weren't meant to go it alone. We were meant for a relationship with God. Through Christ, that sweet connection is restored. He is the One who will help us. He promises us that if we love Him, He will work all things for good. He will redeem all things. He alone has the power to make the sweetest lemonade out of the sourest of lemons.

What a promise. What a prayer!

---

*Father, thank You for taking what is miserable and tragic and working it
for good through Your power and sovereignty. Help me to
trust in Your promises. Amen.*—AH

Hurters or Healers?

"A new command I give you: Love one another. As I have loved you,
so you must love one another. By this everyone will know
that you are my disciples, if you love one another."
JOHN 13:34–35

We have a choice each morning as we wake up to a new day. Will we be the kind of person who causes more hurt in the world, or will we be healers? Will we be a battering blow to someone's spirit instead of a blessing? Will we choose love when it's easier to hate? This choice is ours with every word we speak. Every action we take. Every thought that passes through our minds. For everything has an effect.

Everything.

The Lord's command is to love one another. How hard can that be? Pretty hard when it comes to loving the unlovable. To be honest, loving prickly folks—not you and me, of course—well, it's as easy as giving a porcupine a big bear hug. Not pleasant.

But God can make possible what appears impossible to man. Through prayer, the Lord can help us love those folks who appear unlovable.

So what will you choose to be when you get up in the morning to a new dawn—a hurter or a healer? The world has an overabundant supply of the former and a serious shortage of the latter!

God, give me the strength and patience to encounter the world with the
abounding love of Christ. Help me to love as You love. Amen.—AH

Heavier Than I Can Carry

"For my yoke is easy and my burden is light."
MATTHEW 11:30

Kids are so honest. Don't you love their direct, unguarded approach to life? It's refreshing to see, since as we grow up we tend to become more closed off and less open and vulnerable with other people, with God, and with ourselves.

For instance, if a child is walking alongside her dad at the beach, and she is trying to carry a full bucket of wet sand, most likely she will turn to her father easily, happily, and expectantly to say, "Daddy, can you carry this? It's too heavy for me."

That is how our Father in heaven would like us to come to Him in prayer. We weren't created to carry the heavy burdens of this world. We were made for better things, for loftier things—for joy and peace and love and laughter. For harmony.

So, when we are burdened in this life, let us take on the guileless honesty of a child. Let us turn to Him and, like the little girl, say to God, "Daddy, this is too heavy. Can You carry this for me?" Then we can let it go, whatever *it* is, into His hands—easily, happily, and expectantly.

Father, please take away my heavy burdens. Just as a child trusts her earthly father, help me to trust You with every aspect of my life. I give it all to You. Amen.—AH

Got Prayer?

The LORD is near to all who call on him,
to all who call on him in truth.
PSALM 145:18

Prayer is communicating with God. Wow, really? You mean, we can connect with the Creator of the universe like He's our best friend, only better? Yes, that's it. Sounds unbelievable and more than a little audacious, doesn't it? Yet it's what God desires of us. A sweet and holy rapport. A relationship. Communion.

Still hard to grasp? Perhaps the concept seems so inconceivably wonderful and so simplistic that man feels a need to add to the process, give it his own style, and do it his own way. Perhaps even conjure up his own gods. Yet man cannot change what God has ordained. It would be like filling our car's gas tank with a fuel mixture from miscellaneous liquids we found in the garage, which would, of course, ruin the car for any good use.

Maybe it's easier to explain what biblical prayer is not: Prayer is not meditation. Prayer is not happy thoughts or wishful thinking. Prayer is not sitting in a certain position and clearing one's mind. Prayer is not chanting, visualization, or communicating with a spirit guide.

Prayer is talking directly to God, through Jesus Christ. It is indeed that simple. That intimate. That inconceivably wonderful!

Got prayer?

Creator God, help me to grasp the beautiful simplicity of prayer.
I want an unceasing, rich communion with You,
my Lord and Savior. Amen.—AH

The Prisoner's Prayer

If you declare with your mouth, "Jesus is Lord," and believe in your heart that God raised him from the dead, you will be saved. For it is with your heart that you believe and are justified, and it is with your mouth that you profess your faith and are saved.
ROMANS 10:9–10

We are all prisoners on death row. Yet Christ, with His sacrifice on the cross, has thrown open the cell door for us. All we need to do is walk through. Take His hand as He walks us through the iron gates, the tower with armed guards, the concrete barriers, the barbed wire, and out into the beautiful blue sky of redemption.

Why do some people insist on staying in the confines of a prison cell when beyond the walls of sin is freedom? It comes down to one tormenting word. . . Pride.

Pride keeps us paralyzed; it keeps us fooling ourselves. Pride allows us to accept the lies of Satan: that we are better off on our own, calling our own shots. How else can we convince ourselves that a dark and cold dungeon is better than the pure warm light that streams through the window?

Once again, Christ has already broken our chains. He's opened the prison door. All we need to do is walk though.

The prisoner's prayer of freedom is on our lips. It is written in our hearts by the Holy Spirit. Will we stay or step out into the warm rays of redemption?

Heavenly Father, I believe that Jesus died for my sins and that He is Lord. Please forgive my rebellion and come into my heart. Amen.—AH

The Voice of Heaven

*Jesus answered, "I am the way and the truth and the life.
No one comes to the Father except through me."*
JOHN 14:6

The world says, "What can you give me?" God wants us to say, "How may I help you?" The world says, "I need more." God would like us to say, "I am content. Let me share what I have." The world says, "I can make it on my own. I can save myself." God would like us to say, "Lord, You made me. You're the Way, the Truth, and the Life. Let's walk this dusty road together."

The world never seems to be in sync with what God wants for us, dreams for us. We get the idea that what the fallen earth has to offer is more fascinating and glorious and irresistible. Yet how can that be, when people fail us and everything that *can* fall apart *does* fall apart? When even the kings and queens of this earth are destined to the same lonely and hopeless end without divine assistance?

There are no answers in this earthy dust, only in the voice of heaven. We should look up to our hope—for it lies in Christ and Christ alone. He is life, not death. He is the most fascinating and glorious and irresistible hope there ever was or ever will be. This could be our heart praise as dawn arrives and as the sun sets.

*God, You are the answer to the riddles and the problems of life.
You are the salve for my sin-sick soul. Amen.—AH*

Do You Believe in Miracles?

Now while he was in Jerusalem at the Passover Festival,
many people saw the signs he was performing and believed in his name.
JOHN 2:23

Jesus asks us to believe in miracles. Do you?

Sometimes when we pray, we go away, believing nothing will happen. Maybe our heart prayer should be as the boy's father in the Bible who exclaimed, "Lord, I believe. Help my unbelief!"

God does answer every prayer. It just may not fit our agenda. The answer might come as a "yes," a "no," or a "wait." When miracles do come, it is easy to forget as the Israelites did, even though they witnessed miracle after miracle after miracle. Still, they doubted.

That is the nature of man.

So, let us keep a prayer journal and write down the answers to our prayers, the miracles we experience. They do happen. The journal will be a reminder that God is listening. That God does care about our comings and goings. That He is still all-powerful and able to perform signs and wonders. When the miracles do come, write them down. Praise Him for them. Tell others. From time to time, we should go back and read the journal, see the long list of His tender mercies, so that we might be encouraged.

What miracle are you praying for today?

Lord, don't let me forget the countless prayers You have answered.
Don't let me doubt the power of prayer. Amen.—AH

Too Easy

Isaac prayed to the LORD on behalf of his wife,
because she was childless.
GENESIS 25:21

I know several families right now who are making the same request Isaac made. "God, please, please give us a child." It's the kind of prayer that can be prayed for weeks, months, and years on end, or the kind that comes all at once, rushing in like some desperate wind.

For Isaac, it all seemed so simple. He prayed. God answered. His wife became pregnant with not just one baby, but two! So what are we to tell all the people who are still waiting for their answer? What are we to tell the ones who never get a baby of their own? Have they just not tried hard enough? Perhaps they didn't say the right words or maybe God just doesn't think they would be fit parents.

Or maybe it's just not that easy. Some people pray and seem to get the answers they wanted. Others seem to get handed a harder pill to swallow. I don't think we can know all the plans God has for us.

What we can know is that God is in control, that He hears us, and that He loves us. And the best thing we can do for friends praying for a child is not to try to come up with some explanation for why their prayer has or hasn't been answered. The best thing is just to keep praying with them.

Lord, help me to remember that Your answers
aren't always easy ones. Amen.—ML

Thunderstorms

Ask the LORD for rain in the springtime;
it is the LORD who sends the thunderstorms.
ZECHARIAH 10:1

I'm afraid when it comes to rain, we can all be fair-weather friends. Many people love a gentle, warm sprinkle. But cold, spitting droplets on a November day is enough to give a person a migraine.

In the dry, hot days of summer, everyone is likely to plead with God for rain. Farmers need it for their crops. Children want to play in it and be refreshed. Gardens are crying out for help with their wilting leaves.

But the rain most of us have in mind is probably something along the lines of a quiet, steady shower. We don't necessarily want the driving, violent thunderstorm.

The God who opens the heavens to give flowers a drink is also the God who sends crashing thunder and streaks of lightning. It is good to be reminded of that.

Our God is gentle and warm. Our God is big and powerful. Praise Him for all of who He is.

Lord, thank You for speaking to me in gentle whispers and in strong proclamations. Please help me to honor You always. Amen.—ML

Big Ears

Evening, morning and noon I cry out in distress,
and he hears my voice.
PSALM 55:17

A child once was asked to draw a picture of God. She drew an old man with a long white beard, striking blue eyes, and humongous ears. When asked why God's ears were so large, the girl replied, "God listens to everyone all the time around the whole world. That takes big ears!"

Aren't you glad God has big ears? That He is able to listen to us all the time, no matter where we go or what time of day it is?

David wrote in Psalm 55 of a time of tremendous personal stress. "I am distraught" and "My heart is in anguish within me," he said (vv. 2, 4). Why was he in such trouble? He reveals the answer in verses 12–13: "If an enemy were insulting me, I could endure it. . . . But it is you, a man like myself, my companion, my close friend."

Betrayed! Is there any kind of trouble that causes more worry and heartache? Betrayal gnaws at us day and night—there is no end to the wondering why and the self-doubt.

Thank goodness, God has big ears. We can take our heaviest burdens to Him and He will hear us. Only He can silence the voices of doubt and despair in our heads.

"As for me, I call to God, and the LORD saves me" (v. 16). Yes, David. Us, too.

Lord, thank You for Your big ears! Amen.—ML

In All Circumstances

Rejoice always, pray continually, give thanks in all circumstances;
for this is God's will for you in Christ Jesus.
1 Thessalonians 5:16–18

To-do list: Go to grocery, pay bills, see about plumber, take kids to practice, pick up kids from practice, dentist, cancel appointment, text friend, pray, make dinner, put laundry in washer, walk dog, go to bed.

Is prayer even on your to-do list? More often than not, we all forget to set aside specific time for prayer. Perhaps it gets put off until there's quiet in the house, until we are not so tired, until our work is done, until. . .

It is good to remember that we don't even have to set aside a certain special time. We don't have to sit in a prayer chair or wear a prayer robe. Our God is always there for us. We can talk to Him anytime. Indeed, we should.

Let's go back to that to-do list—how might your day go with prayer as your inner sound track? *God, thank You that I have so many choices of foods to eat. Help me feed those who are hungry. Thank You for the income we have. Thank You for the skills and talents of others. Thank You for healthy kids. . .*and on and on and on.

It's good to have special times set aside for rest and reflection. But it's also good to remember you don't have to wait until then.

Lord, thank You for always being there for me. Amen.—ML

All of the Above

For the LORD gives wisdom;
from his mouth come knowledge and understanding.
PROVERBS 2:6

Every day is full of so many decisions—from the time we wake up till the time our eyelids drop heavily at night, we are faced with decisions both small and significant. *What should I wear? What should I have for breakfast? What am I going to do today? What am I doing with my life?* It's easy to get overwhelmed, even before your Wheaties have a chance to get soggy.

It's also easy to fall into the trap of thinking that if we simply pray about an issue, God will give us the answer—and in fairly short order. Because God knows we need all the answers when we need them, and not a moment later. Right?

It seems that often when we want an answer, the only thing that will do is the answer we want. Nothing less. Yet God, our generous Father, has something better in mind. We want a solution; He wants to give us the formula. We want a simple yes or no; He wants to give us time to see if we even asked the right question. We want A, B, C, or D; He wants to give us all of the above.

Thank You, Lord, that Your ways are higher and wiser and better than mine. Help me to be patient when I lack wisdom, and to see Your knowledge and understanding. Amen.—ML

Prayer of Complaint

*"What have I done to displease you that you put
the burden of all these people on me?"*
NUMBERS 11:11

Have you ever felt the weight of the responsibility of guiding, teaching, leading, and encouraging others? This point in Moses' story is just one of many when he became frustrated with those complaining Israelites. He must have longed for his days as a shepherd, when he could just give the animals a poke or two with his staff to get them to go in the right direction. This Israelite flock was a different story—disobedient, fickle, petty, and selfish. Basically, a normal group of human beings.

Moses knew what to do. He did what he often did when feeling overwhelmed—he talked to God. No, his prayer wasn't pretty—it wasn't full of praise and honor. One might say he was even a little snarky—"Did I conceive all these people? Did I give them birth?" (v. 12).

Chances are, you've voiced your own prayer of complaint a time or two. And you know what? God didn't crush you. God knows our hearts. He knew Moses' heart. Before Moses even began his rant, God saw his need and heard his plea. So the Lord gave Moses the answer he needed—friends. "They will share the burden of the people with you so that you will not have to carry it alone" (v. 17).

*Lord, help me remember to call on You first when I'm feeling
overwhelmed. Thank You for being my friend. Amen.—ML*

Accepted

The Lord has heard my cry for mercy; the Lord accepts my prayer.
PSALM 6:9

The machine quietly whirs. It eats the paper, slurping it up like a mechanical frog pulling in a fly on its tongue. You wait. And wait. Some ticking and chinking and clunking are heard. Then the wrinkled slip of faded green comes rolling out again.

Denied.

What is it about those money-taking devices on vending machines and at the self-pay cash registers that so easily angers a person? Maybe it's the feeling of rejection. You willingly submit your hard-earned cash as a trade for a parking ticket, or a can of soda pop, or, yes, a large hunk of brightly wrapped chocolate that you really, really need. Right now.

But no. No joy. No simple acceptance of the offering. No chocolate.

Thanks be to God for accepting what you give Him. Even when your prayers are feeble, or not well spoken. Even when perhaps all you can do is cry. Even when low blood sugar is talking and you say angry words. God hears you and accepts your prayer.

The machine quietly whirs. The paper once more gets eaten by the mechanical mouth. But this time, it disappears for good. A satisfying clunk is heard as the desired object is dropped down, and then you receive it.

Accepted.

Thank You, Lord, for accepting my prayer, even when I don't exactly know what to say. Thank You for listening to me. Amen.—ML

The Beggar King

"Hear the supplication of your servant."
1 Kings 8:30

Solomon was a wise king. He had all the power of Israel in his hands. He built a magnificent temple, which he was chosen by God to build. He decided hard cases for his people and had riches that were the envy of the world.

Yet in his prayer to God, he sounded like a beggar.

Supplication is not a word that gets used much these days. It comes from a Latin root that means to plead humbly or beg. It's not the kind of action you would expect from a powerful monarch. Yet the Bible is full of unlikely people doing unexpected things.

Over and over in his prayer, Solomon humbled himself and asked for God to hear, to act, and to forgive. He didn't place himself above God or ask for things he did not need. He didn't highlight his own achievements or the greatness of his people. Rather, he focused heavily on their potential downfalls and their sin.

Standing before the "vast assembly" of Israel, he showed his people exactly who was in charge, who was taking care of them, and who they should count on. Not him. Not Solomon the king. But the Lord, the God of Israel. For "the LORD is God and. . .there is no other" (v. 60).

God, there is no one like You. Help me to show others that anything good in my life comes from You, and nowhere else. Amen.—ML

Less Is More

"They devour widows' houses and for a show make lengthy prayers."
MARK 12:40

When did quantity start being valued over quality? It probably goes back to ancient times. One guy starts collecting rocks. Another guy makes a bigger pile of rocks. And on it goes.

Greed is what makes people keep grabbing for more. That feeling of wanting what you cannot really ever hope to get on your own. The feeling of being powerless and needing something—and lots of it—to fill the void.

The teachers of the law were afflicted with this disease. They had a measure of respect and power, but they wanted more. It was not enough for some of the people to acknowledge their greatness—they wanted everyone to do so. They must have known that the real power and honor and wisdom was nothing they could claim.

So they wore long robes, and took long strides, and sat at long tables, and voiced long prayers—all to show that they deserved respect.

Just after Jesus comments about these teachers devouring widows' houses, we see Jesus sitting down, watching the crowds bringing their offerings. From the hands of the rich and powerful came large, showy quantities of coins. But a poor widow gave only a couple of pennies.

"Truly I tell you," Jesus said, "this poor widow has put more into the treasury than all the others" (v. 43). The lesson was clear.

Lord, please make me humble. Help me to use my words
and actions to point to You, instead of myself. Amen.—ML

Comfortable

Praise be to the God and Father of our Lord Jesus Christ, the Father of compassion and the God of all comfort, who comforts us in all our troubles, so that we can comfort those in any trouble.
2 CORINTHIANS 1:3–4

A goose-feather-filled duvet. The purring cat curled up by the crackling fire. The aroma of chocolate chip cookies baking in the oven. Soft rain on a cloudy day, a good book, and a cup of tea.

Everyone has their favorite sources of comfort. When a workday hasn't gone well, or a rather large bill has arrived, a fight has occurred, or a loved one is suffering, people reach out for a security blanket—in the form of a person, place, or thing.

Humans need that tangible reminder of safety, peace, and strength. It starts from the moment those little bodies burst out of the womb and into the foreign air. The cries go up, the hands reach out, and tiny fingers grasp for anyone who will bundle them up and make them feel they are not alone.

God loves us so much, He feels our worries and bears our troubles, and reaches out to us through His words and His songs and His reminders of love, that come in all the little ways He knows will suit us best. He comforts us through the hands and feet of others who embrace us in hard times.

Lord, help me to be a comfort to others in the ways You comfort me. Amen.—ML

Lies

If a ruler listens to lies, all his officials become wicked.
PROVERBS 29:12

"Oh, be careful little ears what you hear." Have you heard that song? It was taught to little children in churches many years ago. The song is about protecting your heart by monitoring what goes into your ears and eyes and so on. Generally when someone talks about protecting your ears, they are talking about things such as bad language, or dirty jokes, or, perhaps, wrongheaded theology. Yet many people, whether rulers or not, would do well to heed this proverb.

This proverb paints an interesting story in just one line. Imagine that the once-respected, once-popular ruler, perhaps weighted down with daily decisions, seeks advice from someone. Someone she trusts but who has not earned her trust. Someone wise by worldly standards, someone who knows how to please. This someone spins tales in her ear, stories of triumphs and treasure, of winning respect and arguments and. . .votes.

Once the ruler listens to the lies, her officials see that lying is the way to be heard. You see, they don't start out wicked. They "become" wicked—because they realize that is the way to get attention, to gain power, to find a listening ear.

Yet what would have happened if the ruler had been listening to truth instead? What would have happened if the ruler had spent more time listening to God in prayer?

---

*Dear Lord, help me to remember to listen to You
and not just talk. Amen.—ML*

Grocery Prayer List

For from him and through him and for him are all things.
To him be the glory forever! Amen.
ROMANS 11:36

God, thank You for the produce: for bananas and grapes, and carrots and cucumbers. Thank You even for brussels sprouts and for the lowly potato. Thank You for an abundance of crops and healthful foods. Thank You for the men and women that farm the land and take care of the orchards, for the ones who pilot the boats and planes and tractors and trains, for all the people involved in harvesting this food, so shoppers can buy a fresh pineapple for ninety-nine cents on sale.

God, thank You for the people who care for the livestock that produce the meat we eat, and for the fishers who gather the bounty from the sea. Thank You for many hours of hard work that go into producing all the ingredients so cooks can create the perfect meat loaf.

Thank You for milk that nourishes little bones and teeth, and helps everyone grow. Thank You for all the milk substitutes, and that for every dietary need these days, there is, somewhere, a product that will satisfy.

Thank You for the household goods in plentiful supply. Especially for toilet paper, Lord. Thank You for toilet paper. Enough said.

And thank You for convenience foods that make life a little easier, for doesn't everyone once in a while need to make dinner in just one minute and fifteen seconds?

For all these things, Lord, we thank You. Amen.—ML

Body Talk

If the whole body were an ear, where would the sense of smell be?
1 CORINTHIANS 12:17

One big ear. Can you imagine it? If everybody walking around your neighborhood today did not have hands and feet and noses and bellies, but just one big ear? It seems like some kind of Daliesque nightmare. Body piercings would be even more prevalent. Wax removal would be big business. And just imagine the size of the Q-tips!

Thanks be to God that we are not all giant ears, but that instead people have many parts. And indeed, that as one body in Christ, there are many different kinds of people, with many different kinds of gifts and abilities.

At times it seems life would be a lot easier if everyone could think and talk and walk alike. But if you've ever been a part of a team of people working toward a common goal, you know how valuable it is to have members of the team be able to contribute in different ways to the different aspects of the work.

So if today you are annoyed by someone, perhaps someone who is quite different from you, try to imagine what life would be like if everyone was the same. Then be thankful for the differences you encounter—even the annoying ones. Just think, it could be a lot worse. You could be shopping for giant Q-tips!

Lord, thank You for Your amazing creative powers.
Help me to appreciate every person as a part
of Your creation. Amen.—ML

It Takes an Army

*David went down with his men to fight against
the Philistines, and he became exhausted.*
2 SAMUEL 21:15

In 2 Samuel 21, David is king—not the shepherd who killed Goliath and frightened away the Philistine army with a single stone. He is an older man and cannot endure the rigors of battle.

Isn't it comforting to know even King David became exhausted? Sure, he was fighting a battle against powerful warriors and not just doing laundry. But stain fighting is hard work, too, right?

Once again, a heavily armed and vengeful Philistine threatened David's life. One of David's men killed the warrior. Then David's men decided their king's life would not be endangered again. "Never again will you go out with us to battle, so that the lamp of Israel will not be extinguished" (v. 17).

In biblical context, kings could make any laws they wanted and rule as they saw fit. But a king without an army is a sitting target. Without an army to support and protect him, David would have died on the battlefield that day.

Have you thanked God today for the army of supporters that allow you to accomplish your work? Have you thanked the friends and family members who look out for you, protect you, and give you a chance to rest? If you haven't, go ahead. Put down this book and do it now.

*Thank You, God, for all the people who help me
survive every day. Amen.*—ML

A Warning

Do not be arrogant, but tremble.
ROMANS 11:20

In Romans 11, Paul delivers this rather stark warning. He has been talking about the Israelites, and how they did not receive all the blessings they could have received because of their disobedience. He reminds the Gentiles to not feel as though they are superior simply because they have been granted salvation—a place of standing in the family of God. No, instead he encourages them to remember that they are just a branch of a very old and long-standing tree. Just as God has pruned the tree before, they are vulnerable to trimming as well. It is only through faith, which comes from God, that any people can belong to the Creator of all.

Can you think of any people today who act as though they own the market when it comes to true Christianity? That they are the real Christians, and others are just lame imitations? If you've lived long enough, you will know that just about every person who ever called on the name of the Lord has at one time or another made the mistake of thinking they were the only ones who knew how to pronounce that name just right.

Tremble at the almighty power of our great God, who gives, and takes away, and gives again out of His abundant grace. Let us strive to be so generous.

---

*Dear Lord, help me be more filled with faith
than I am with criticism. Amen.—ML*

Award-Winning Laziness

A sluggard buries his hand in the dish;
he is too lazy to bring it back to his mouth.
PROVERBS 26:15

Wow. Did a picture just form in your head? A picture of the person who would win the Laziest Person Ever Award (though of course, the winner would be too lazy to come and claim it)?

It's a beautiful piece of description. You can just see the person. Sitting there at a table laden with goodies, his rolls of fat piling up over his belt. He reaches a swollen hand into a casserole, grabbing a piece that would feed a family of five. He sighs heavily, as if even exhaling takes an effort. His arm hangs limply, balanced on the edge of the table. What will he do? Will he eat the casserole? Will he keel over from cholesterol overload?

Before your mind goes on painting this lovely picture, you might want to take a look in a mirror.

God has given you tremendous blessings—a world full of gifts to enjoy, good work to do, family and friends to love, and a grace that knows no bounds. Yet how many of us sit there at His table with our hands just lying in the plenty, refusing to do the work of faith required to receive what God has in store? Avoiding reading His Word, forgetting to pray, pretending that faith is not a discipline, but just another dish on the table.

Lord, help me not to be lazy in my pursuit of You. Amen.—ML

Preparations

Always be prepared to give an answer to everyone who asks you to give the reason for the hope that you have.
1 PETER 3:15

Painting is like many manual jobs in that a good deal of the work involved in this task happens in the preparations. Selecting the paint, buying the paint, buying the tools, clearing out the furniture, cleaning the surfaces, taping up the areas not to be painted, laying down the drop cloths, priming the surfaces, letting them dry, stirring the paint, setting up a ladder, and pouring the paint. Finally, after all of that (and no doubt you expert painters out there will note any steps left out), you paint.

The same is true for telling others about your faith in Christ. People often feel nervous or reluctant to talk to people about their faith, and it seems likely that part of that has to do with a lack of preparation. If you practice your faith daily by talking with God, studying His Word, talking with other believers about questions you have, and serving others, you will feel more confident about describing what your faith is all about. It will be easier to give the reason for the hope that you have if you are actually living in that hope every day. Why not begin your preparations right now?

Dear Lord, thank You for the hope we have through Jesus Christ, Your Son. Amen.—ML

Seeker Friendly

"If you seek him, he will be found by you."
1 Chronicles 28:9

Somewhere in the nineties, the seeker-friendly trend began to grow among Christian churches. The idea was to craft worship services that were not exclusionary, but that would welcome and appeal to masses of people who either did not know God at all, or just were not regular churchgoers. This trend manifested itself in different ways, depending on the church. For some people, *seeker friendly* meant incorporating secular pop music or film clips into the service. For others, *seeker friendly* meant just opening the church doors.

Whatever way it showed up, the idea was, people needed help to seek God. They couldn't find Him on their own. Now, there is too little space here on this page to argue the ins and outs of or whys and hows and reasons seeker-friendly services are or are not good ideas. But one thing seems pretty clear from scripture:

God is seeker friendly.

He is not hiding from you. He is not turning His back on you. He is not a bouncer at the gate, judging you based on what jeans you are wearing or how many tattoos you have or whether you drink. He welcomes all who are seeking to find Him. The details will get sorted out later.

Lord, help me to seek You every day. Amen.—ML

A Conversation

"Simon son of John, do you love me more than these?"
JOHN 21:15

There's a beautiful recording of an example of prayer in John 21. It's a conversation that takes place between Peter and Jesus, after Jesus had risen from the dead and had appeared to His disciples. Three times in the conversation Jesus asks Peter about his love for Him, and three times He gives Peter a command to take care of or feed His sheep.

People often have similar conversations with God in prayer. God asks something of you, and you respond. He asks again, and you respond again. He asks again, and so on. If you're honest, you'll admit that there's probably a good reason you keep hearing the same question asked of you again and again.

Let's face it—Simon Peter isn't exactly pictured as the tender-loving type in the Bible accounts that include him. He's more of a go-getter, a doer of the Word, not a lover of the people. So it's not surprising to hear Jesus pressing him on the subject that was likely to be a point of weakness for him.

So what is Jesus pressing you about? What question have you heard God asking you over and over again? What has your response been? Better yet, what will it be?

Dear Father in heaven, thank You for our conversations.
Help me to constantly listen for what You have to say to me. Amen.—ML

Call to Action

"We must obey God rather than human beings!"
ACTS 5:29

"I don't wanna."

"Do I have to?"

The struggle for obedience is as old as the idea of chore lists. Whenever humans are faced with a requirement, we have a natural bent toward disobedience.

Here Peter shouts out a call to action through the centuries. "We must obey God rather than human beings!"

Now, any teenagers who happen to read this should take note: Peter does not say we should *dis*obey human beings—particularly your parents.

It's just that when it comes to following the orders of men and women or following God, the choice should be a no-brainer, right? Let's not kid ourselves. The choice isn't always that easy to figure out. Sometimes people might even find themselves following someone who claims to be speaking the Word of God, only to discover the person was really speaking lies.

When Peter shouted this out, he was facing a very real possibility of being put to death for proclaiming Christ. Odds are, not many now reading this book will face such an extreme situation as Peter's. Yet it should encourage us to keep stepping forward. If Peter can face death and still obey, people today should be able to face discomfort and do likewise.

One last thing to note about Peter's call—he didn't shout alone; the apostles were replying together with him. You're not alone, either.

Dear Father God, help me to obey You every
step of the way. Amen.—ML

Commanding Presence

Trouble and distress have come upon me, but your commands give me delight.
PSALM 119:143

Not often does a person in trouble look up from her sobbing and cry, "Please, somebody, give me some commands!"

The word *commands* is not generally seen in a positive light. Commanding someone sounds too authoritative, too bossy, and too pushy. People don't want to be commanded—they'd rather be guided, led, or called.

Yet God commands. When people come into His commanding presence in prayer, they do find comfort. Why? Because when the foundations of your life are shaken, you want to hold on to something that is real, that is true, that will not and cannot be moved. The law of the Lord is that. Moreover, His law is *good*.

The more you meditate on His Word, the more you'll be convinced of this. God's laws for living together and loving one another are evidence of a mind high above ours—a mind not hampered by a constant focus on self. Use the laws of God in your prayer time, and you will be forced to think about others, to consider what it means to really live in community, and to put others before yourself. In that process, the sorrow and trouble that is weighing you down will not disappear, but will be put in proper perspective, and thus, become a little bit of a lighter load.

*Lord, thank You for the comfort
You bring us in Your law. Amen.*—ML

Without Punishment

The punishment that brought us peace was on him,
and by his wounds we are healed.
ISAIAH 53:5

If you are a caregiver to children, you will have witnessed the relief that punishment can bring. A child does a bad thing. That child tries to cover up aforementioned bad thing. The child becomes increasingly miserable and or mired in more trouble as the deceit rises to ridiculous proportions. Finally the child is punished, and after the required amount of sobbing, yelling, or complaining has been achieved, the child goes and plays in peace. All is right with the world. . .for now.

In each of us is a built-in, God-created desire for justice. We want good to win over evil. We want wrongs to be made right. We want no bad guy to go free. Even, as it turns out, if that bad guy happens to be us.

When we pray and ask for peace, it would be good to remember we are asking the One who created peace—the only One through whom our peace can ultimately come. Only Jesus can give us that. It is by His wounds we are healed, no one else's. His wounds are our punishment—a punishment we would not have been able to bear. God loves us so; He wanted us to be able not just to survive, but to live eternally.

Dear Jesus, thank You for taking on what we could not.
Please help us to live to understand Your peace. Amen.—ML

Be Quiet

"In repentance and rest is your salvation,
in quietness and trust is your strength."
ISAIAH 30:15

This verse sounds lovely. . .until you go on: "but you would have none of it."

These are the words Isaiah relayed to God's "obstinate children." They could just as easily be directed to any of us today. The words of the Lord speak of people who "carry out plans that are not [his]," and heap "sin upon sin" (v. 1). They are "children unwilling to listen to the LORD's instruction" (v. 9), who ask their prophets instead to "tell us pleasant things" (v. 10).

How easy it is to fall into the bad habit of relying on our own way! There are hundreds, maybe thousands, of books each year published with the sole purpose of helping us to help ourselves. They teach us to distract ourselves with compliments and inspirational fluff. God compares this kind of living to the creation of a wall that is "cracked and bulging," not able to stand up under its own weight. So it collapses. Yet it doesn't just fall down. It crumbles into such a worthless heap that not even a bit of it is functional (vv. 12–14).

So, how do you fight this result? God gives us the answer. Through repentance and rest, quietness and trust. You won't find a better way to develop those qualities than through daily prayer.

Dear Lord, help me to trust You and to want to
see through Your eyes. Amen.—ML

Grace

When you have eaten and are satisfied,
praise the LORD your God for the good land he has given you.
DEUTERONOMY 8:10

Repetition can be a very good thing. For those of us who are growing older, it can be the only way of hanging on to our memory of names, places, dates, our own birthday, and so on. Some people place a picture of a special person or event in a place where it can be seen every day, and every day the picture serves as a reminder to be thankful for that person or opportunity.

How many times do you eat in a day? Three, maybe more? Do you pray each time before you eat? Maybe we should wait, as Deuteronomy 8 suggests, and pray afterward, thanking God for the good He has given to us.

Perhaps you aren't in the habit of praying at all with meals. However, there is definitely a reason for it. Moses points it out here in the following verses: "Be careful that you do not forget the LORD your God. . . . Otherwise, when you eat and are satisfied. . .then your heart will become proud and you will forget the LORD your God" (vv. 11–12, 14).

So use your mealtimes as reminders, as a picture of all the good opportunities God has given you. Eat, and remember. Drink, and remember. Be satisfied, and remember. Pray, and remember.

Dear Lord, thank You for this food, and for the people who made it,
and for You, who made everything.—ML

Worried Sick

The mind governed by the flesh is death,
but the mind governed by the Spirit is life and peace.
ROMANS 8:6

Do you worry? Ahem. Perhaps a different question is in order. What did you worry about today? This morning? In the last hour? Goodness knows there's enough in the news to drive people to bite every single nail off their poor hands, if they could only stop wringing them long enough to get a nibble.

Yet a life of worry is not the life our Father had in mind. It's not really a life at all. "The mind governed by the flesh is death." Here Paul is more likely speaking of a spiritual death, but a physical death is just as likely. A mind that is overcome by the body's physical desires and needs will not be a mind that can focus on the path to Christ. These desires and needs can produce mental distress (*What will I eat?*) or they can actually worry the mind to a frazzle, like a dog worrying a bone to a saliva-soaked, useless lump.

So what does this mean? Don't care about physical needs? Ignore our desires? Don't worry, be happy? No, just don't be ruled by these things. Don't let the striving for physical satisfaction or the emotional desire for calm cause you to neglect the daily maintenance of spiritual health.

The Spirit is life and peace. Pray daily for more of the Spirit and less of the flesh.

Dear Lord, help me to trust in You and ask You
for all that I need. Amen.—ML

The Unbeliever's Prayer

The boy's father exclaimed, "I do believe; help me overcome my unbelief!"
Mark 9:24

This prayer could be called "The Parent's Prayer." Is this not the cry of every mother and father? Perhaps especially so for those who have children going through the suffering of chronic illness, mental illness, addiction, school struggles, and spiritual battles.

Let's be honest: none of us would want to deal with this father's struggle for more than an hour, let alone years. It's bad enough that his son has an unexplained condition that doesn't allow him to speak. Every parent knows the frustration of trying to figure out what a prespeech toddler wants or doesn't want—generally while he's in the middle of a piercing scream that could wake the dead. Yet here is a child who periodically throws himself into harm's way—"into fire or water to kill him" (v. 22). We can guess who has been there every time to save his boy from being burned or drowned.

This father believes there is a cure, an answer. Why else would he come to see Jesus? At the same time, this man is tired. He has been disappointed so many times. It is not hard at all to understand his cry for help. Anne Brontë echoed this feeling in her poem, "The Doubter's Prayer":

> *Without some glimmering in my heart,*
> *I could not raise this fervent prayer;*
> *But, oh! a stronger light impart,*
> *And in Thy mercy fix it there.*

Dear Lord, help me believe more. Amen.—ML

Exposed

*He will bring to light what is hidden in darkness
and will expose the motives of the heart.*
1 CORINTHIANS 4:5

Have you ever replaced lightbulbs in a room? Listen to the voice of experience: don't do this while company is over. Suddenly every dust bunny, every finger smudge, every piece of lint is exposed for all the world to see. No, it's better to do this well before your visitors arrive, so you have time to do something about it. Or, just take the lightbulbs out again, light some candles, and call it mood lighting. Who cares if it's only four in the afternoon?

When would you like your secrets brought to light? In what setting would you like the motives of your heart laid bare? Why not ask God to reveal truth to you in the quiet and privacy of your own conversations with Him?

When you pray, ask God to bring to light the sins you have forgotten that day. Ask Him to point out things that you haven't even realized you are struggling with. Paul said, "My conscience is clear, but that does not make me innocent" (v. 4). Just because you think you are on the right path doesn't mean you've never taken a wrong step. Ask God to turn on the lights and reveal the weak points in your faith.

But then, don't be surprised if what you see is a messy room!

*Dear Lord, shine Your light on my heart so I can be
a better witness for You. Amen.*—ML

Like a Tree

Blessed is the one. . .whose delight is in the law of the LORD,
and who meditates on his law day and night.
PSALM 1:1–2

Sometimes the best thing you can do when you take time to be with God is simply to meditate on His Word.

When you are tired, it is good to be reminded that His Word endures. When you are weak, it is good to remember His Word is strong. When you are confused, it is good to remember His Word has answers. When you have been hurt, it is good to know His Word can heal.

A tree has no choice about where it is rooted. Through a turn in the wind or the whim of a bird or the thought of a gardener, a seed is planted in the ground. Then year after year the tree grows there (or doesn't). The tree cannot go for a walk or visit other grounds. So a tree planted by streams of water is blessed indeed. That tree gets the benefit of life-giving liquid along with the changing scenery the stream brings under its boughs each day.

So a person who delights in God's Word is blessed by it. It gives life, and it brings an unending array of characters and circumstances to your mind, without you ever having to take a step. You can stand strong in the knowledge of God's commands and still experience a wealth of opportunities—and prosper!

Dear Lord, thank You for Your Word. Amen.—ML

Not Your Battle

"All those gathered here will know that it is not by sword or spear that the LORD saves; for the battle is the LORD's, and he will give all of you into our hands."
1 SAMUEL 17:47

Have you ever been involved in a really ugly fight? Harsh words are hurled on both sides, personal attacks are launched, people pick sides, and soon it seems your whole world is at war.

But that battle that you are fighting? It isn't yours. So lay down your weapons and squelch the fires of vengeance. Pack up your war horses and get down on your knees instead.

David was in an ugly fight. Goliath was not exactly a humble opponent. He was big and loud and mean and scary. The Israelites were not showing themselves to be especially brave at the time. So David, the shepherd, stepped into the middle of this mess armed not with swords and catapults and spears, and not even with a sling and a stone. No, David was armed with the strength and power and might of the living God.

You are, too. Perhaps you haven't seen God rescue you from the paw of a lion or bear, as David had. Yet you can be confident that God is more than able to get you through whatever challenge you are facing. Spend some time with Him. Ask Him to help you. Place your battle in His capable hands.

Dear Lord, please let me lean on You. Amen.—ML

Pillow Talk

In peace I will lie down and sleep, for you alone,
LORD, make me dwell in safety.
PSALM 4:8

It's happened to the best of us. You wait until the house is all quiet to spend some time with the Lord. You grab your Bible, you get your notebook. Your pen is poised over the page as you wait on the Lord. You open your mouth a little as you begin your prayer. You breathe deeply and relax as you list the ways you are grateful that day for God's help and blessings.

Your Bible slips a little down your comforter. Your notebook pages crumple. Your pen rolls to the floor. Your mouth opens broadly as the snoring begins. You breathe deeply in heavenly sleep as you dream about God's blessings. . .or something like that.

A mind stilled in prayer can easily become a mind stilled by sleep. That's okay. At least, some of the time. You wouldn't want your prayer time to end up being nap time every day. Yet one of the benefits of a relationship with the Maker of heaven and earth is the peace that comes from nowhere else. It's better than any super, high-tech mattress or the latest ultraessential oil.

In the peace that comes with prayer, you can lie down and sleep, knowing God is watching over you.

You alone, Lord, make me dwell in safety. Amen.—ML

Abba

Because you are his sons, God sent the Spirit of his Son into our hearts, the Spirit who calls out, "Abba, Father."
GALATIANS 4:6

Did you have a special name for a father or grandfather when you were little? Perhaps it's a name you still use to this day. Saying that name can conjure up all kinds of memories—portraits of an intimate relationship with one you love, and who loves you.

God wants to have that same kind of close relationship with us. He loves us more tenderly and patiently than even the best of fathers here on earth. He has adopted us as His own, making us brothers and sisters of Jesus Christ. Jesus called out to His Father in the language of His childhood—Abba—so we can call on our Father God and expect the same intimacy.

Indeed, God has given us His Spirit to live within us. It's a mystery. Yet if you've ever been in a hard spot when you couldn't even really think how to pray, you have probably felt closer to understanding this mystery than at any other time. It's at those times you can almost hear the Spirit's voice whispering for you, calling on God on your behalf, asking for help when you can't even form the words.

How amazing that the Creator of the universe allows us to call Him "Daddy"!

Abba, Father, thank You for making me Your child. Amen.—ML

The One Who Lifts

But you, Lord, are a shield around me, my glory,
the One who lifts my head high.
PSALM 3:3

Down. Depressed. Dejected. Droopy. In the dumps. Disappointed.

Some days there is no use trying to hide it. You are just sad. It may be something has happened recently to make you feel this way. It may be an old sorrow that has come to mind. For some, it may be no reason at all—just some concoction of chemicals in the brain is out of whack and your happy mood is the casualty.

Whatever it is, God is ready and willing to protect us from ourselves. Just read Psalms for a little while and you will see the psalmist was often not a happy camper. In fact, he could be a bit of a downer! At least he knew where to turn for help: "But you, Lord, are a shield around me, my glory, the One who lifts my head high."

God is able to lift up your spirit, your mood, your hopes, and even your chin. Remember to glory in Him, particularly when you are not feeling so glorious. He will answer. He will put a shield around you. He will absorb your sorrow and lift your head up out of the gloom.

Dear Lord, please help me to know You are always with me,
even on my sad days. Amen.—ML

A Prayer to Arms

Finally, be strong in the Lord and in his mighty power.
EPHESIANS 6:10

Dear God, help me to know my real enemy—not my annoying neighbor, or my demanding boss, or my fickle friend. Help me to recognize the powers of this dark world when they come at me, and help me not to waste my time fretting over little offenses that mean nothing. Help me to think bigger, to see broader, to know more of Your wisdom.

Help me to stand my ground.

God, make my tongue speak Your truth. Wrap Your Word around me tight like a belt—help it to hold all things together. Please mold for me a guard around my heart, so that I can long to follow Your righteous path and not the desires of this world.

Make me ready, Lord, with answers to those who ask questions and wonder about You. Help me not be afraid to speak, but to be confident in my replies because I know You are behind every word of the Gospel of peace.

Make me strong, so I can bear Your shield of faith, repelling insecurities and fears and doubts that are the weapons of my enemy. God, You know the words and thoughts and actions that sting me the most. Please help me let Your peace and the certainty of You be a salve on my soul.

Fill my head and heart with Your Spirit so I can go out and pierce others with the security of salvation in You. Amen.—ML

Morning Routine

In the morning, Lord, you hear my voice; in the morning
I lay my requests before you and wait expectantly.
PSALM 5:3

Dog owners are often greeted by their companions in the morning, with eyes full of expectation. The request of the dog is quite clear— take me on a walk, please! It is certain that dogs are the most energetic waiters in the animal kingdom. Even a well-trained dog, while seemingly sitting patiently, has every muscle fiber in its body just straining to be released. Why is this? Because it is certain, with not a shadow of a doubt, that very soon indeed it will be allowed out. It will be let go. It will run.

Maybe you wait for the Lord's answers in the same way. But many of us do not. Do you ever lay requests before God morning after morning (or night after night), going through the routine, but not really believing God will come through?

Oh, to be like an expectant dog! Waiting for God's response to our prayers with eagerness and readiness to spring into whatever discipline or action God requires. Waiting with certainty, sure that our Father will answer soon. Waiting with utter trust in the Master, because we know He has our best interests always in mind. Waiting expectantly.

Dear God, help me to have confidence and faith to ask You anything,
and to wait eagerly for the reply. Amen.—ML

Wrong Number

"Go and cry out to the gods you have chosen.
Let them save you when you are in trouble!"
JUDGES 10:14

Reading the book of Judges is like watching some kind of soap opera for the nations. First the Israelites love God, and then they don't. Then they do. Then they don't. Then they do. . .you get the picture.

Judges chapter 10 starts off calmly enough, but then we get to verse 6: "Again the Israelites did evil in the eyes of the LORD." Our writer then proceeds to list no less than seven different groups of gods that the Israelites decided to serve, instead of the one and only Lord God. After the Israelites get crushed by the Ammonites (one of the people groups whose gods they were worshipping) and start feeling distressed, they suddenly remember to call on the only name that matters.

Does this sound familiar at all? Things are going pretty well. Your basic needs have been met and now you want more. So you start chasing after ways to get it: money, power, position, image, people, leisure, and insert-idol-name-here. Somewhere in the middle of that chasing you stop becoming a worshipper of God and start becoming a worshipper of other stuff. You forget who you are. You forget who to call on.

Thanks be to our merciful Savior, who is always there for us. Even when we call the wrong number.

Dear God, thank You for loving me even
when I'm unfaithful to You. I'm so sorry. Amen.—ML

Success

Then he prayed, "Lord, God of my master Abraham,
make me successful today, and show kindness to my master Abraham."
Genesis 24:12

How often do you pray for job success? Perhaps a promotion or a raise or some sort of recognition?

How often do you pray for God to show kindness to your boss?

Imagine if the CEO of a corporation sent his top executive out on a matchmaking mission for his own son! That would seem like a fairly trivial matter in today's business terms. Back in the age of Abraham, the family *was* the business. So Abraham sent his most important servant—the one in charge of everything he owned (which was a lot, in those days)—on this very important mission. This servant was the only one he could trust to do the significant and delicate negotiation required to obtain a good wife for his son, who would carry on the family business.

The servant knew the weight of his responsibility. He wanted to do well, not just for himself, but for his master and his master's family. So he prayed. He asked God to help select the right woman for Isaac. God did not let him down.

Next time you are handed an important mission, remember to ask the ultimate CEO for help. Ask to do well, not just for yourself, but for your boss and for the whole company. God will not let you down.

Dear God, thank You for good work
and the will to do it. Amen.—ML

Flood

The LORD has heard my weeping.
PSALM 6:8

Flash flood alert. Psalm 6 has a rather high humidity level. The psalmist is in anguish, down to the bone. He has flooded his bed with tears and drenched his couch. Next thing you know, his friends will be filling up sandbags around him.

We've all been there. Something happens that just breaks your world apart, and the tears start coming. Then they won't stop. You think they will never stop. You think you will just go on weeping until you haven't a drop of water left in you, at which point you will be so overcome with dehydration, you will just die. Then what?

Isn't it somehow comforting to see the psalmist throwing himself on his couch in utter misery? To know that thousands of years ago, bad days—really horrible ones—happened? To know that in the end, the same Lord and God who soothed and saved that poor, miserable, soaking wet psalmist lying on his couch is the same Lord and God who soothes you today?

Our God is an expert on human suffering. He's had centuries of experience in counseling people through grief of all kinds. So the next time you feel like the tears just won't ever stop, come immediately to the door of the best counselor you could ever find. Come in prayer. Come with a box of tissues. Just come.

Dear God, thank You for hearing my sobs
and not turning away. Amen.—ML

Watching from the Reeds

Then she placed the child in it and put it among
the reeds along the bank of the Nile.
EXODUS 2:3

There is very little emotion captured in the story of baby Moses. A woman has a baby. She can't hide him from the cruel government, which legislated his death, so she puts him in a basket in the river. No tears. No sound. The end.

It wasn't the end, thankfully, for baby Moses. It's hard to imagine that was the end for his mother, either. Even after her daughter followed the baby boy, watching him be rescued by royalty; even after she finished nursing her son and gave him back to be raised by his adoptive family; even after the boy had grown up and fled the land—it seems likely that it wasn't the end of the story for Moses' mother.

How many mothers are there out there who have watched from the reeds and prayed? First, that their babies might be rescued, might be saved from whatever terrible set of circumstances they were born into, and might be given a chance to grow and live. Then, that their babies might continue to thrive, to become healthy adults. Maybe one day, to know that their mothers loved them.

Say a prayer today for those mothers watching from the reeds.

Dear Lord, thank You for the gift of life. Please bless all those mothers
who have made sacrifices so their babies could survive. Amen.—ML

The Pit of Negativity

Whoever digs a hole and scoops it out
falls into the pit they have made.
PSALM 7:15

Sometimes those hoarder shows on television are fascinating, though disturbing, to watch. It's amazing to listen to and observe people who have almost dug their own graves. The walls made of stuff are literally falling in on them. Their lives are held together by piles of old memories, regrets, longings, and disappointments. The need to be filled by something they cannot find has left them empty, while their houses are stuffed to the rafters.

Any one of us can get stuck in the pit of negativity. It's so easy to do. One self-pitying thought leads to another, and then leads to an irritation with others, which leads to more exclusion, which leads to more jealousy, which leads to more irritation and isolation, and the cycle continues.

Instead of digging holes, let us work to help each other out of them. Let's give thanks for what we have, instead of counting what we don't. Through our prayers and worship "sing the praises of the name of the LORD Most High" (v. 17). It's very hard to dig a hole if you keep looking up.

Dear Lord, help me to not get trapped by negative thoughts.
Fill me with Your Spirit. Amen.—ML

Want. Ask. Get.

You do not have because you do not ask God.
JAMES 4:2

It seems so simple. Want. Ask. Get. James breaks it down for us. He says, "You desire but do not have, so you kill. You covet but you cannot get what you want, so you quarrel and fight. You do not have because you do not ask God" (v. 2).

What is it you are afraid to ask for? What is it you are afraid to admit you need? Maybe you just need help. Maybe you need the truth. Maybe you need a loan. Maybe you need to be saved. Maybe you need to let go.

Want. Ask. Get.

What is it you really want? Not just a new car or more money or a nice outfit. What is it you're lacking that makes you want what others have? Do you want what God wants for you? Do you even know?

Once you know what you want, how do you ask? Do you look everywhere else first before coming to God? Do you go to Him right away? Do you come to Him humbly or as someone entitled?

You want, you ask—did you get it? If your answer is no, have you thought about why? What were your motivations? What's your reaction to not getting what you want?

If your answer is yes, have you thanked God? Have you shared what you have? Want. Ask. Get. Then give.

Dear God, help me to make Your desires
for my life my own. Amen.—ML

Bargain

It is better not to make a vow than to make one and not fulfill it.
ECCLESIASTES 5:5

"God, if You just give me a puppy, I'll be good my whole entire life." How many children must have prayed a prayer like this one? How many of us are still praying this kind of prayer?

People make promises to God for all kinds of reasons, but most likely the biggest one of those reasons has to be to strike a deal. "God, if You'll _____, I will _____."

It is good to think of God as your friend. It is dangerous to think of God as your haggling partner.

Besides, He would be the worst person ever to bargain with. Why? He doesn't need anything. When you are trying to strike a deal, it's best to know what your counterpart needs—what he or she lacks that you can offer.

The God who made time, who spun the earth into motion and placed the stars in the sky, does not need you. He does not need anything you have to offer. He does not need your promises. Especially the empty ones.

He does want you to come to Him. He does want to be near you. He does want to love you. He will give you everything you could ever need. Come near to God, and He will come near to you. Not to negotiate a deal, but just to know Him more.

Dear Father, if You'll love me,
I will have everything I need. Amen.—ML

Helper of the Fatherless

*But you, God, see the trouble of the afflicted; you consider their grief
and take it in hand. The victims commit themselves
to you; you are the helper of the fatherless.*
PSALM 10:14

Too many children know this grief—the gut-wrenching sorrow of losing a dad. Some have watched their fathers suffer and die. Some have watched their fathers walk away. In either case, the hole that is left behind is gaping.

Losing a parent shakes a person's foundations. Both sons and daughters feel this loss keenly, though perhaps somewhat differently. For sons, it is the loss of a role model, a strength giver, a provider, a teacher. For many daughters, losing a father means all of that, but also losing the first and perhaps the only man in the world who would truly love them no matter what. The one man who would always look at them—no matter how many pounds were on or off, or if it was a bad hair day, or if a pimple had erupted—and say with absolute honesty, "You are beautiful."

God sees your troubles, and He knows your pain. When you come to Him in prayer, He cradles you in the palm of His hand because He is that big. Big enough to take on your sorrow. Big enough to lift us all. Yet close enough and gentle enough to wipe your tears and whisper, *"You are beautiful."*

*Father God, thank You for never leaving me.
Please hold on tight. Amen.*—ML

Humbled

*We all, like sheep, have gone astray, each of us has turned to our own way;
and the LORD has laid on him the iniquity of us all.*
ISAIAH 53:6

When you come to God in prayer, do you ever feel the complete humbleness of your situation? It is a truly humiliating experience— not that God makes us feel how little we are, but that being near God makes us see how little we are.

Perhaps that's why we don't do it as often as we should. It's not comfortable to feel shame.

We are sheep. We run away. We ramble. We get off track. We lose our way. We chase after the wrong things. We fear everything. We cry out and complain. We can't find our way home. We are stubborn. We don't see well. We don't ask for help. We stumble.

Our Lord and Shepherd knows all of this, and loves us still. He knows all of our wrongs, and He doesn't just forget them, or wipe them away. He pays for them. In blood.

That is the God to whom you say your bedtime prayers.

*Dear God, I am humbled in Your presence.
Help me to live a life that is worthy of Your love. Amen.*—ML

What to Do?

"When the foundations are being destroyed, what can the righteous do?"
PSALM 11:3

Anyone who has ever owned an old house knows what a worry a cracked foundation can be. Sometimes it can be repaired. But a foundation that is weak means the whole house will likely have to come down, or else, it will eventually fall down.

The psalmist in Psalm 11 asks a good question. What can the righteous do? When the whole stability of a world is crumbling, when the people who are supposed to be upright are being corrupted, when everything that is supposed to be true turns out to be false—what can the righteous do? What should they do?

We might come up with many answers. Worry. Shout. Look for someone to blame. Use the trouble as an excuse to give up. Hurry up and build a new house.

But the psalmist doesn't tell the righteous what to do. He tells them where to look. "The LORD is in his holy temple; the LORD is on his heavenly throne" (v. 4).

When the foundations are shaken, look to the One who cannot be shaken. Look to the Lord, who is "righteous, he loves justice; the upright will see his face" (v. 7). Turn your face to God and ask for His help. Turn your eyes toward Him, and remember who is in control.

Dear Lord, help me in times of trouble to remember to turn to You in prayer. Amen.—ML

Forming

We are the clay, you are the potter; we are all the work of your hand.
ISAIAH 64:8

People have a romantic vision of the potter: the potter spins the clay on the wheel, and a few moments later, a beautiful pot is formed. Voila!

But anyone who has worked with clay or watched a potter knows it's not that easy. Here's how it might go: The potter puts a slimy lump of clay on the wheel. The potter spins the wheel. The potter uses fingers and hands to start forming the lump. A beautiful shape begins to appear. The vase starts stretching up, up, and then—oh no! It folds over in a sad, twisted bow.

The potter begins again. The vase stretches up, and then, well, a little over. A little up. A little more over. The potter sighs in frustration, squashes the crooked vase, and starts again.

The ball forms into a bowl. The potter's hands smooth the rim of the bowl. The potter sneezes. A large dent appears in the rim of the bowl. The potter stops the wheel and goes to get a cup of coffee.

We are the clay. Thankfully, we are in the hands of a perfect Potter. Yet the process of our spiritual formation can still be frustrating and longer than we wish. It will take daily prayer and lots of patience for us to wait and stretch up and up and up—into a functional vessel.

Dear Lord, may my prayers help me to be formed by You. Amen.—ML

Transforming

*And we all, who with unveiled faces contemplate the Lord's glory,
are being transformed into his image with ever-increasing glory,
which comes from the Lord, who is the Spirit.*
2 CORINTHIANS 3:18

If you are like most people, you will find fault with at least one aspect of your image. It's hard to find anyone who is completely happy with the person she sees in the mirror.

It would be harder still to find anyone who is completely happy with the person she is—with all the decisions and thoughts and actions she has made in her life. Or even just today.

Thanks be to God, "where the Spirit of the Lord is, there is freedom" (v. 17). No one has to hide from the Lord. No one has to worry about the exterior image. No one has to feel alone.

If you have been running away from God for a while, or just neglecting your prayer life, it's time to turn and face Him. He does not expect you to be perfect. He expects that you will need transforming. He is happy to perform that work. He wants to shape you into the best human being you can be. Come and kneel before Him; don't hide your face. He can see through any veil you might try to wear anyway. Come and stand before His image and ask Him to transform you.

---

*Dear God, I'm not happy with who I am.
Please mold me into the person You want me to be. Amen.—ML*

How You Should Pray

"When you pray, do not be like the hypocrites."
MATTHEW 6:5

There are not that many places in the Bible that spell out exactly how people should perform the Christian disciplines of faith. Jesus' words in Matthew's Gospel come as a welcome relief to those who are seeking to know exactly how to behave as a follower of Christ.

First, He paints a picture of what not to do. Don't pray to be seen. Don't use prayer as a step on the faith success ladder. Don't think you have to be seen for the Father to hear your words. Don't look for any reward or praise outside of the glory that comes from God Himself.

Do not babble on, using words as a weapon of power or as a show of strength. Don't think that God desires quantity over quality. Don't make the mistake of thinking God needs to hear you speak at all.

Instead, pray quietly. Pray on your own. Pray in private. Pray with words that show God respect, that show you know His power. Thank God for His provision. Ask Him to forgive what you lack. Request His guidance and His salvation. Ask Him for His will to be done, even if you have no idea what that is just yet.

Then go out and live as you pray. Be forgiving, knowing your Father has forgiven you, time and time again, for all the small and big ways you have stumbled.

Our Father, in heaven, let Your will be done. Amen.—ML

Fast

"When you fast, do not look somber."
Matthew 6:16

People engage in all kinds of fasting fads these days. Juice fasts. Cleansing fasts. TV fasts. Fasting has become a status symbol of sorts. It's a true sign of a society that has plenty when people have the option to choose what they will declare as a fast.

For other people in the world, fasting is sadly just a way of life.

Yet fasting was meant to be a kind of prayer. The idea is to deliberately go without something (usually food) in order to focus on God and on His will for your life. It's a time to be reminded of who provides everything we eat and drink. It's a time to be reminded of who we depend on and who we can trust with all of our needs and desires. Often it is meant to be a time to bring a particular desire or concern before God.

The fasting is not for God. It is not a show for others. The fasting is a very personal decision to engage in a small act of sacrifice, and in so doing remind yourself of the much greater sacrifice God has made for you.

So if you do fast, don't make a show of it. Don't advertise it. Do it with a right heart and mind, and God will certainly honor your efforts.

Dear God, help me to focus on You more,
no matter what else is going on in my life. Amen.—ML

Faithful

If we are faithless, he remains faithful, for he cannot disown himself.
2 TIMOTHY 2:13

Is there anyone who has not been unfaithful, at one time or another? Not to a spouse or dating partner, or even a friend—not that kind of unfaithful. Perhaps there are people who have remained true in all of those situations.

But unfaithful to God—has anyone managed to escape that label? It seems unlikely. For many of us, the challenge would be to find a time when we *aren't* unfaithful. Even one whole day when we remain focused on His will—when we take charge of our thought life and all of our actions and remain obedient to Him, every hour. When we remember to praise Him and thank Him for what He has given. When we don't get distracted by other objects of our desire—idols we have worshipped before.

God is gracious. He is faithful—forever faithful. He cannot deny Himself, and thus, He cannot deny His love for us. He will always be there for us, even when we stray far, far away. If we come to Him in prayer, He will always respond. For that, we can be thankful. For that, we should be faithful.

Gracious God, thank You for always being true to us,
even though we are not worthy. Amen.—ML

Mary's Glory

"He has been mindful of the humble state of his servant."
LUKE 1:48

What is striking about Mary's prayer in Luke 1 is the confidence. Here is Mary, a young girl in a completely unheard-of situation. She is carrying the child of God in her womb. Strange and wonderful things are happening around her. People are having experiences and dreams and hearing from God in ways they never have. Mary receives Elizabeth's blessing with all the composure of a woman five times her age.

It is clear to see this confidence does not come through the mind of a teenager, ruled by emotions and hormones. It comes from a deeper place. "My soul glorifies the Lord and my spirit rejoices in God my Savior" (vv. 46–47). Mary knew she was not anything special on her own. She knew also, from deep within, that God was doing something great, not just for her, but for generations. In the same way she had heard as a child the stories of the amazing things He had done for her ancestors, she could see with certainty the Lord's hand at work now in her own time, her own village, her own body.

Let us come to God and praise Him with the same certainty Mary had. Let us read His Word and remember His marvelous works. Then let us pray with a humble heart and ask Him to open our eyes to the work He is doing today, in our world, in ourselves.

My soul glorifies You, my Lord. Amen.—ML

What Are Your Gifts?

*Each of you should use whatever gift you have received to serve others,
as faithful stewards of God's grace in its various forms.*
1 PETER 4:10

Were you born an artist? A painter, writer, or sculptor? Do you gravitate toward the sciences? Are you gifted in sports? Floral arranging? Speaking? Computers? Sales? Building? Organizing? There are so many talents.

What about your spiritual gifts—such as teaching, prophesying, showing mercy, serving others, encouraging, and leading?

Some people are confused about their abilities, and they might even think they have been passed over when the Almighty was giving out gifts. Yet, we can be assured that everyone has been given talents, and everyone is expected to use them.

If you are questioning what yours are—ask God. The Lord will be more than pleased to tell you. Asking for His guidance concerning our talents and spiritual gifts is also wisdom, since God wants us to use them with a servant's heart. Even though that notion might seem old-fashioned within our modern mind-set, it is how Jesus conducted Himself—with the heart of a servant—when He walked among us.

*God, thank You for the gifts and abilities You have blessed me with.
Help me not to waste them or use them for my own gain but to serve
others with my talents in order to glorify Your name. Amen.—AH*

When Prayer Seems Impossible

LORD, save us! LORD, grant us success! Blessed is he who comes in the name of the LORD. From the house of the LORD we bless you.
PSALM 118:25–26

Sometimes the last thing on earth we feel like doing is praying.

We're angry. We're scared. We're exhausted; we're world weary.

Maybe we've just had an argument with a close friend. Maybe we've just been admitted to the hospital with yet another debilitating illness. Maybe we are bone tired from working two jobs and still not making the rent. Maybe we feel as though our prayers are never heard. That we are truly alone. That life seems hopeless.

What in the world do we do?

Pray.

Yes, even then. The book of Psalms is full of every manner of heart cry to the Almighty. Nothing is held back. Every tear is shed in those passages. Every weary thought is revealed. Every doubt and misery expressed. And what happened? God listened. He came near. He became the people's Rescuer and Redeemer. As in Bible times, God may not choose to lift us out of every storm, but when we cry out, He will be there with us, whether it's in a howling gale or a still, blue sea.

Prayer is mighty because the One to whom we pray is mighty. Let us never forget.

*Savior, please be with me in my hour
of need and bring me hope. Amen.*—AH

I Will Give You Rest

The LORD replied, "My Presence will go with you,
and I will give you rest."
EXODUS 33:14

The world is full of clamor and shouts and unsavory whispers. Our attention is stolen at every turn. Even Christians can absorb and reflect the noise if they're not careful. They can take in that frenzy, that panic. That soul-wrenching fright.

Christ did not come to give us a spirit of fear. He did not come to condemn, but to save. He came to give us a rich life in spirit and truth. He came with healing in His hands. He came with redemption and mercy, love most abundant.

Let us rest in these truths—rest in Him.

The Lord reaches out to you. He will take you by your outstretched hand and lead you to a restful place. By still waters that lap gently to the shore. A place that is far from the roaring crowds. Far from the clamor of fear. From the whispers of temptation. From the accusing cries of the enemy.

Yes, the Lord says, *"My presence will go with you, and I will give you rest."*

Can you hear His gentle voice? He's calling us to sit a spell. To visit. To rest.

Father, amid my trials and frustrations today, give me rest and peace in You.
No matter how difficult my circumstances may be, help me to remember
that You are more than capable and sufficient for me. Amen.—AH

Chapel Bells, Tolling for Thee

"They sing to the music of timbrel and lyre;
they make merry to the sound of the pipe."
JOB 21:12

Stained-glass, arched windows, and a steeple adorn a pure white chapel on a distant hill. How beautiful. How peaceful. How heartening. And the bells, oh how pretty are those chapel bells that ring out through the vales and through the villages to gladden every heart who hears their music.

It is a reminder to see beyond the mundane. Downturned faces will once again rise from the daily tedium and toil and witness the firmament—the swirling clouds, azure sky, and stars of night that shout His glory!

The tolling bells call to me and to you—as a reminder to gather together in worship, to seek, to fellowship, to share communion, to praise, to pray. To return to all the things—and the One—who is easily forgotten, easily set aside.

The bells ring of hope. Those in Christ have great reason to make merry, to shout in joy, to sing to the music of all kinds of instruments.

When we hear the chapel bells, let us remember to look up. To gather in worship. To raise our voices in song. To embrace the hope. And to prayerfully and excitedly share that hope with all who will listen.

Lord, You are worthy of all praise. I want to worship You every day,
every hour, and every moment. Amen.—AH

Sweet to the Soul

If we confess our sins, he is faithful and just and will forgive us our sins and purify us from all unrighteousness.
1 John 1:9

A boy sneaks a big sugar cookie from Mom's cookie jar just before suppertime.

Does the boy sit at the table, calmly looking around, munching on the sweet treat innocently?

Probably not.

Most likely—since he knows his mother asked him not to eat a cookie before dinner because she loves him and wants him to eat a healthful dinner first—the boy will do what many boys do and hide in his room with his guilty pleasure.

The boy's mother—since she already knows about the incident, because she really does have eyes in the back of her head—hopes that he will confess his folly. Would it really be that hard to come to her and say, "I'm sorry, Mom. I shouldn't have eaten the cookie. Will you forgive me?"

Repentance may feel uncomfortable, but only for a short time. Usually Mom will forgive with a gentle warning and a hug.

God's love is far beyond our own, so we are safe in His perfect justice and mercy. We need not run and hide in our folly, but go to Him instead. He is faithful and just and will forgive us our sins. Yes, repentance is such sweetness to the soul.

Father God, I come to You now with all my sins, both intentional and unintentional. Thank You for Your unlimited grace. Amen.—AH

Pride Is a Wily Beast

*Better to be lowly in spirit along with the oppressed
than to share plunder with the proud.*
Proverbs 16:19

We've seen it. We've experienced it. It makes our hearts shudder.

Pride. Pride doesn't sweep in on a cloud of French perfume. Pride slithers in brazenly yet craftily and is as pleasant to endure as breathing deeply from the mouth of an open grave. Oh, my! That image offends our more delicate sensibilities. But so does pride, which can settle itself into our spirits—if we allow it to—as we relish good fortune such as money, accolades, physical beauty, knowledge, fame, and so forth.

These potential conduits of arrogance seem obvious, but pride is a wily beast, since the opposite of good fortune can conjure it up just as easily. We can choose haughtiness when we know we've risen victorious in our suffering. When we know we are able to endure—even invite—great hardship and lack. You mean we can choose to feel prideful in poverty? Yes, it can come when we least expect it and for any reason. That's why pride is so sly as well as insidious. In the book of Proverbs, God says that He detests the proud of heart.

Uh-oh. Not good. Then how can anyone cleanse oneself from this putrid pride?

With the power of God through prayer. He will cleanse us from all unrighteousness, including pride, and the results will smell sweeter than the finest French perfume.

*God, take me down from my pedestal and teach me
the meaning of true humility. Amen.—AH*

Looking for Trouble

Finally, brothers and sisters, whatever is true, whatever is noble,
whatever is right, whatever is pure, whatever is lovely, whatever is admirable—
if anything is excellent or praiseworthy—think about such things.
PHILIPPIANS 4:8

Here's the scene. . . .

You have lunch with your dear friend, Tallulah, and you both are having a nice time together, yakking about all the latest news in each other's lives. The usual catching-up stuff. Then you hug and say good-bye. Yet on your way home, your mind begins to pick apart—every—single—word—that was said during your lunch. You pick and pick like a vulture—until you rise up from the now dead carcass of a luncheon—with a morsel of questionable meat. Aha! Yes, you now know positively that Tallulah has slighted you in some way with something she said at lunch. Or might have said. Or might have meant. Maybe.

We women are notorious with this pick-pick thing. Are we not? The bottom line is, if we're looking for trouble, we will find it. Guaranteed. That's life. So, instead of picking, let us give each other one of the best friendship gifts—the benefit of the doubt. Let us pray this beautiful Philippians scripture aloud.

"Whatever is true, whatever is noble, whatever is right, whatever is pure,
whatever is lovely, whatever is admirable—if anything is excellent
or praiseworthy"—Lord, please allow me to think
about such things. Amen.—AH

How Beautiful Is Thy Name!

*All flocks and herds, and the animals of the wild, the birds in the sky,
and the fish in the sea, all that swim the paths of the seas. LORD,
our Lord, how majestic is your name in all the earth!*
PSALM 8:7–9

When we experience an alpine walk along a misty trail. Or take in the moon's reflection on a still blue sea. When we hear the thunderous roar of a lion, or the voice of the wind through swaying palms. Or when we see the ballet of the dolphins, or the glistening fire of a rare gem, or the artwork in the plumage of a peacock, don't we feel a rush of awe? Don't we feel a sweet ache in our hearts to be thankful—to Someone?

God's creation is indeed full of beauty and wonder, and we should take great pleasure in His handiwork. We should explore His world. We should see with new eyes each morning. To delight in the smallest of snowflake designs to the vaulting cliffs on the grandest mountains.

As Christians we do not worship creation, but we instead worship the One who is the Creator of such magnificence. A thankful heart full of praise is a form of prayer. Shall we thank Him and praise Him today?

Lord, our Lord, how majestic is Your name in all the earth!

*Creator God, thank You for the beauty and wonder of Your handiwork.
Give me grateful eyes to see it every day. Amen.—AH*

Don't Forget to Smile

"By this everyone will know that you are my disciples,
if you love one another."
JOHN 13:35

Religious bondage. Maybe you know some folks who are suffering with this spiritual ailment. They're the ones who are so busy wringing their hands they forgot to raise them in praise. If someone is hungry and asks for bread, they're the ones who divvy out a stone; because the stone will help the needy learn endurance. They're also the ones who forgot how to laugh or smile or encourage, because they're obsessed with trying to make certain that no one breaks a rule. Ever.

Yes, you guessed it—they're the prune gang.

Oh, dear. Sounds like the same pharisaical struggles in Bible times. What about the unbelievers in our midst? What will they think? Who wants a faith that looks oppressive? They'll be lacing up their running shoes to get away from us as fast as possible! As Christians we should indeed follow Christ in all things, but that prayerful following should cause us to want to reflect His joy, peace, and love, which He gives freely to us.

If the joy in our hearts is so uncontainable that it's busy spreading itself all over our faces, people will take off their running shoes and stay to chat with us. They'll ask, "What is it that makes you smile?"

Jesus, just as You love me, help me to love everyone around me—family,
friends, and foes. I want to be a perfect reflection of You
to a hurting world. Amen.—AH

We're Meant to Fly

"Come now, let us settle the matter," says the LORD. "Though your sins are like scarlet, they shall be as white as snow; though they are red as crimson, they shall be like wool."
ISAIAH 1:18

Suppose there was a beautiful white seagull that suddenly got caught in a patch of sticky mud, but the more the poor thing struggled to fly, the more the mire coated its wings and held it down. Got that image in your imagination?

How is that different from our daily walk on this earth? We as humans were meant to fly free of worry and disease and suffering and death. This fallen journey is not what God had planned for us, but it was instigated by humanity through the choice that God gave us—which is free will. Our spirits weren't meant for these immense burdens. They are almost unbearable at times.

Wow. Sounds pretty hopeless. It is completely hopeless without the love and sacrifice of Jesus. Only He can fulfill the promise in scripture that says He will make our sins, which are scarlet, as white as snow. No one else can do it. No other gods. Not our own desperate efforts at redemption. Nothing.

His promise is real, and with His redemption comes freedom. It's like being released from the mire—yes, clean and white, wings outstretched, and soaring!

What will your prayerful reply be to His promise? His redemption?

Jesus, thank You for Your priceless sacrifice on the cross for my sins. Help me to soar free from the taint of sin. Amen.—AH

Words Gone Bad

May these words of my mouth and this meditation of my heart
be pleasing in your sight, Lord, my Rock and my Redeemer.
Psalm 19:14

There's a fuzzy, ripe peach in the grocery store, and it has your name on it. It's juicy, fragrant, and sweet as candy. You tenderly bring it home and set it in the bottom of your crisper in the fridge. And then you promptly forget about it.

Uh-oh.

Well, that same luscious, fuzzy peach will soon be covered over with the ugliest and fuzziest green monster mold you have ever seen, making it impossible to eat. Impossible for anything of good use. That is the way of words gone bad.

Once our words are spoken, once they have tumbled out of our mouths, we can never get them back. They are like the water that plunges from a cliff into the sea. It just keeps on going, flowing and changing everything it touches. That water cannot come back. Our words cannot come back into our mouths. Yes, we can apologize and make amends. We can ask the Lord to forgive us, and He will keep His promise. Yet the sting of those thoughtless remarks can sometimes last a lifetime—in the recipient's heart as well as in our own spirits.

A helpful daily prayer would be to ask the Lord to temper our words with wisdom and love. That what we say will not go bad like a rotten piece of fruit. But that our words will be pleasing and good and usable in His sight!

God, help my words to always be kind,
compassionate, and uplifting. Amen.—AH

No Shrinking Violets Here

"Have I not commanded you? Be strong and courageous.
*Do not be afraid; do not be discouraged, for the L*ORD
your God will be with you wherever you go."
JOSHUA 1:9

When the world says, "Boo," do you jump? It's very hard not to. Right? Our days can be arduous, and our nights riddled with terrors. Our spirits grow bone weary and our hearts skittish and faint. So, when people mean to harm us, or Satan comes to attack us, we feel like running to hide in a safe little closet or crawling in bed and pulling the covers over our heads for a day.

Or a month.

Until we sense that life has decided to settle down. But the problem is, just as soon as the wave of suffering is over, we see another storm brewing on the horizon. How can we ride these relentless storms for a lifetime and make it safely to the shores of heaven?

Reading God's Word, staying connected to a Bible-believing church, and praying are the only answers in these perilous times. If we remain faithful to following Christ, we will be able to rise up and say with confidence, "Lord, I will be courageous. I will not fear what the world can do to me. I will not become discouraged, since I know You will be with me wherever I go."

Father, I have complete victory through You. With You on my side,
I have nothing to fear. Help me to fully trust in You. Amen.—AH

Do You Ever Feel Like a Misfit?

For here we do not have an enduring city,
but we are looking for the city that is to come.
HEBREWS 13:14

Do you ever feel as though you don't fit in anywhere? That you're not in sync with the rest of the world? That somehow the earth and its inhabitants are singing a tune you've never even heard of?

Well, that can be a good thing. We are not intended for this world. Our home is meant to be in heaven with God. Reunited with the One who made us, who loves us best.

Yet we certainly try to fit in down here, don't we? We don the finest costumes, whatever is in vogue. We engage in the most practiced and acceptable sounding banter—the popular vernacular of the day. Yes, sometimes we find ourselves dancing to the tune of a fallen earth, which might even include the transgressions we witness all around us.

This city or town or country hamlet of ours is not a forever place for us. As Christians, we are not of this world. We are only passing through. So, the next time we feel as though we don't belong here, know that in a way, it couldn't be truer.

We are longing for home, the home where we will fit perfectly, and the home that will never pass away. Shall we pray for others—that they, too, will find their true home?

God, comfort me when I feel alone and lost in this forsaken world.
You are my true home. Amen.—AH

He Holds the Blueprint

"And even the very hairs of your head are all numbered."
MATTHEW 10:30

We spend our lives searching for someone to understand us, to "get" us. Don't we? When we find it, what a blessing! Yet the understanding we long for comes freely from the Almighty. Even though there are billions of humans on our planet, no two people are just alike. Not even identical twins. We each are uniquely and wonderfully made. It is our loving Creator who holds that blueprint—which He considers precious—that has your name on it.

Imagine God so loving the world—loving us—that His "knowing" extends to the number of hairs on our heads? He knows every single thing about us. The kind of friends we enjoy. Our favorite ice cream, favorite pets, and favorite hobbies. The things that tickle our funny bones. The things that make us cry at the movies. Every secret we've hidden. Our deepest longings. Our worst nightmares. Yes, the Lord knows every nuance and detail about us. He loves us dearly.

Knowing these truths will help us to pray, since being loved and understood by the One to whom we are praying, makes all the difference in the way we begin, "Dear Lord. . ."

Thank You for knowing and loving every single part of me. Help me to run to You when I feel misunderstood or forgotten. Amen.—AH

The Way We Were Created to Be

And do not grieve the Holy Spirit of God, with whom you were sealed for the day of redemption. Get rid of all bitterness, rage and anger, brawling and slander, along with every form of malice. Be kind and compassionate to one another, forgiving each other, just as in Christ God forgave you.
EPHESIANS 4:30–32

As Christians, we have been given a promise of eternal life, but even as Christians, we can still grieve the Holy Spirit who lives within us. When we explode at our spouse and then let the sun go down on that anger. When we say slanderous things about our neighbor. When we make plans that have malicious intent. When we hold bitterness in our hearts toward our best friend. All of these transgressions, and well, any kind of sin, grieve the Holy Spirit. Why? He is perfect love. He loves us enough to help us out of our wayward thoughts and our errant ways. To be perfected in our faith. To be made whole and beautiful.

What a wonderful prayer today, and every day, that the Holy Spirit will make us more like Him. Ah, yes, the way we were created to be!

Holy Spirit, please don't allow my sinful nature to get in the way of Your transforming, sanctifying power. Embolden me to spread the Gospel and love the unlovable. Align me with Your will. Amen.—AH

Where Shall I Pray?

But Jesus often withdrew to lonely places and prayed.
Luke 5:16

Are you searching for the best place to talk to God? One might think of a great cathedral or perhaps a hometown chapel. Or maybe you'd like to be near a quiet stream or sitting under a favorite willow tree with the breeze giving sway to the leaves. What about one's front porch early in the morning before everyone rises or the solitary space of a prayer closet? Fortunately, all of these places work, since God is omnipresent. Since the Lord is all around us, He can hear our pleas and our praises wherever we happen to be. In a crowded bus or a stadium full of people or even an airport terminal bustling with noisy travelers.

We know from God's Word that Jesus often withdrew to quiet places to pray. The culture during Jesus' time—even without anything fast paced or high tech—could still have created enough "busy" to make seeking out a solitary place important. Vital, really.

So, even though we can pray anywhere and everywhere, let us also seek out solitary places to talk to God. We can regain our sense of peace—His peace. To hear His words of guidance. To remember that His power is sufficient for every day, every task.

Where is your favorite quiet place to talk to God?

Lord, help me to carve out pockets of time to seek You in quiet, solitary prayer.
You deserve my complete, undivided attention. Amen.—AH

A Face Lit with Joy

Do not be anxious about anything, but in every situation,
by prayer and petition, with thanksgiving, present your requests to God.
And the peace of God, which transcends all understanding,
will guard your hearts and your minds in Christ Jesus.
PHILIPPIANS 4:6–7

Sometimes when we bow our heads, we feel a little hesitant in addressing God, knowing He is the Creator of all things. It's certainly not the same as approaching our earthly father, or our boss, or teacher or pastor. So, we sometimes approach God with trepidation.

Fortunately, God's Word gives us direction, even in prayer. First, we are not to spend our lives wringing our hands in worry. If we have concerns and requests, we should present them to God and trust Him with the answer. His response might not be what we asked for or on our timetable, but He will be faithful, because He loves us.

We are also to make our appeals with a thankful heart, rather than with a muttering and grumbling spirit, since the Lord is good and He knows how to give good gifts to His children. When we follow these divine instructions, the Lord will give us peace, a peace that is beyond human understanding. It is the kind of calm and sweet serenity that will make all those who meet us ask, "What gives your heart courage, and what is it that makes your face light up with joy?"

Lord, I surrender to You every worry, fear, and burden.
You are more than sufficient for me. Amen.—AH

His Ways

Therefore, in order to keep me from becoming conceited, I was given a thorn in my flesh, a messenger of Satan, to torment me. Three times I pleaded with the Lord to take it away from me. But he said to me, "My grace is sufficient for you, for my power is made perfect in weakness."
2 Corinthians 12:7–9

In his second letter to the Corinthians, the apostle Paul wrote about his thorn in the flesh. We don't know what that misery was specifically—if it was depression, a speech impediment, chronic pain, a spiritual issue of some kind, or something very different. What we do know is that Paul prayed multiple times to be released from this torment. God did respond, but it was with an answer that might have surprised Paul. God said, "My grace is sufficient for you, for my power is made perfect in weakness."

This is a biblical concept that is puzzling, since weakness in a world that values strength seems unacceptable. But God's ways are not our ways—and this truth in tension as one might call it—is His divine view of our struggles, not ours.

Perhaps we could ask this—what if our weakness forces us to slow down and hear God more clearly? What if that struggle gives us more compassion for others? What if that frailty is made perfect as it illuminates God's power rather than drawing attention to man's efforts? This might help us to understand that thorn—even the one that aches in our own flesh.

God, when I am weak and afflicted, give me Your strength. Apart from You I am nothing. Amen.—AH

A Special Window of Opportunity

Then people brought little children to Jesus for him
to place his hands on them and pray for them.
MATTHEW 19:13

People are very willing to tell you their troubles. Over coffee. Over the fence. Over the counter. Over everything. Friends, family, acquaintances, even strangers will sometimes tell you the most private details of their ongoing ailments and travails. Rarely will they refuse you if you say you're willing to pray for them during your quiet time with the Lord. This can be a divine appointment that can be a multifaceted opportunity.

Think of the unbeliever and how an offer of prayer might lead the discussion to spiritual matters, and then provide an opening to mention the good news of the Gospel.

Jesus showed us by example how important it is to intercede for others. Let us pray for ourselves, yes, but let's not neglect the needs of others. A habit of praying for others will cause us to think beyond our own lives, and it will help us lead a more Christ-centered life. The scriptures tell us that the prayer of a righteous person is powerful and effective. What encouragement! What divine assurance!

Who might you pray for right now?

Father, I lift up in prayer the people I have forgotten in the midst
of my own concerns. Grant me compassion as I seek out those who
are hurting and bring their burdens to You. Amen.—AH

Grandstanding

*"But when you pray, go into your room, close the door
and pray to your Father, who is unseen. Then your Father,
who sees what is done in secret, will reward you."*
MATTHEW 6:6

Grandstanding. What a word. It can mean showing off. Yes, we humans
are forever trying to impress others and get that spotlight to swivel
over to us on that grand stage of life. Even as little tykes we begin the
process of learning how to get attention. We wail and wiggle and giggle
and coo and shout and sing and sigh and stomp and put our little fists
on our hips—anything to be in the limelight and show how important
we are. Then we grow up and do adult versions of the same thing.

Bottom line? Humans love attention.

It's safe to say that showing off isn't a deed that is promoted in the
Bible. In fact, Jesus says, "But when you pray, go into your room, close
the door and pray to your Father, who is unseen. Then your Father,
who sees what is done in secret, will reward you."

It's a simple directive. Should be easy, right? It's not that easy.
Perhaps we need a prayer to preface our other prayers and ask God to
make us prayer warriors who carry the sword of truth rather than the
trumpet of pride.

---

*God, help me to remember that when I pray, I should not be seeking the
approval or admiration of others—I should be seeking You alone. Amen.*—AH

The Recordings That Play in Our Heads

Do not put your trust in princes,
in human beings, who cannot save.
PSALM 146:3

If you're human, you've heard the recordings—the ones that play in our heads. Women especially have perfected the art of self-deprecation. You know what I mean—all those cruel remarks that seem to be permanently embedded in our spirits. Such as: *you'll never see that dream come true. You'll never amount to anything. You'll never have a family of your own. You're not smart enough, pretty enough, thin enough. God is mad at you. Nobody loves you. You're pathetic.*

Sound familiar?

The enemy of our souls would like nothing better than to keep us in a hopeless limbo of either false self-confidence or lack of faith in God. So much so, that we can no longer believe the Lord's promises for our lives. Not a good place to be.

Pray that we can have faith in the Lord to empower us to do great things, since the scriptures tell us that we can do all things through Christ who gives us strength. With Him by our sides, we can do all the things we were created to do.

Best advice? Trust God. Delete the recordings!

Lord, it is through You that I find my worth and value.
Shield me from the lies that beat me down. I am Your child—known,
forgiven, and unconditionally loved. Amen.—AH

Better to Endure

"He cuts off every branch in me that bears no fruit, while every branch that does bear fruit he prunes so that it will be even more fruitful."
JOHN 15:2

Oh, how pleasant to see and smell big blousy roses in full bloom—when they are ripe and full and fragrant. Beautiful. The finest rosebushes, the strongest and the healthiest specimens, are those that are pruned scrupulously. Ah, yes, we know where this story illustration is going. No one likes discipline. Not from parents or teachers or police officers or clergymen, or God. It's uncomfortable, and it's embarrassing.

But it's necessary.

How many times have we met children who haven't been disciplined by their parents, who've been given whatever they wanted, whenever they wanted, without any sensitivity to what they really needed? Not a pretty sight. Later, they end up being such miserable adults, that they may even miss out on what they were destined to be.

The Lord wants the best for each of us—and the best sometimes requires that uncomfortable d-word. Discipline. But wouldn't it be better to endure God's occasional prunings than the devil's persuasions and praise? The Lord wants more for us than we can even imagine for ourselves.

Thank God today for His corrections, for they are full of mercy and love.

They are beautiful.

Dear Lord, thank You for always desiring what is best for me, even if it sometimes requires painful discipline. Help me to trust Your sovereignty and love. Amen.—AH

The Black Flood

Out of the depths I cry to you, Lord.
Psalm 130:1

Those black nights. When loneliness becomes like a living thing. When disaster strikes unexpectedly. When you can't seem to draw another breath because the sense of failure or grief or pain seems to consume the very air. The night. The last drop of your hope.

What can you do? Who can you turn to?

God.

He alone is all you need for life and hope on those black nights. He is mighty and powerful and living hope. He is the One who made you, so He knows exactly what you need. Cry out to Him on those black nights. Cling to Him when the world comes crashing in and everyone has fled. When you feel your sin is beyond redemption. When every last drop of hope seems to have dried up. His promises are real. His grace is sufficient. His mercy endures forever. His Word stands. Pray and believe.

He is right here with you. He will never leave you or forsake you. No burden is too great for Him. No sin too dark that He cannot wash it away. He will forgive. He will cradle you in His love. He will reach down and touch your cheek, because He considers you to be His precious child.

Cry out to God. He is right here. . . .

Heavenly Father, help me to cling to You in times of despair and hopelessness. Wrap me up in the safety of Your arms and soothe me with the peace of Your presence. Amen.—AH

Big Talk

Then he continued, "Do not be afraid, Daniel. Since the first day that you set your mind to gain understanding and to humble yourself before your God, your words were heard, and I have come in response to them."
DANIEL 10:12

They say everything is bigger in Texas, but you don't have to live in that big state to experience big pickup trucks. Big hair. Big beef. Big talk. Oww. That last one is as common as mosquitoes in summer and just as unwelcome. Ever been around someone with BIG talk? When that person Won't. Stop. Talking? It's unnerving. And maddening. After a while your brain goes numb, your eye begins to twitch, and your feet get the itch to run.

There are a lot of people in the world who have this problem. They love the sound of their own voices. They believe their words are a spring of wisdom when they're really a fount of NOISE. Even with a pickax, you couldn't chisel your way into the conversation. You begin to wonder, with so many people talking, is there anybody out there who is listening?

God is.

Yes, your words will be heard. He will respond. That is a promise. What will you say to God?

Lord, thank You for listening to me better than anyone ever could. When there is a lack of attentive ears, help me to turn to You instead of despairing. I have found a friend in You. Amen.—AH

When We Think of God

For you make me glad by your deeds, Lord; I sing for joy at what your hands have done. How great are your works, Lord, how profound your thoughts!
PSALM 92:4–5

Do you ever feel the flatness of life—as if you were one of those cartoon characters who's been bopped on the head with a mallet and your head now meets your knees? Do you approach the day with words like these? One-dimensional. Dull. Gray. Dreary. Stale. Tedium. Humdrum.

The God of the universe wants us to start our day with a different mind-set. There is nothing about God and His creation that is humdrum. Nothing. He made the elegant silhouette of a swan. The shimmer of a sunrise on a pristine glacier. The whispers of tropical wildlife still unknown to man.

When we think of God and His creation our words should be transformed. They might become: Mysterious. Exotic. Breathtaking. Radiant. Exhilarating. Enlivening. Miraculous. Prayer is connecting with that mind. That heart. That brilliance. That life and color. That perfection.

Let us come into His presence with thanksgiving and praise. Let us come to know Him who is extraordinary beyond compare. And through that communion, let us see His world and His people as they were meant to be.

Creator God, open my eyes to the richness and vibrancy of life. I want to encounter each day with the freedom and joy that is abundant in a relationship with You. Amen.—AH

Living in the Shadows

"Who can hide in secret places so that I cannot see them?" declares the LORD.
"Do not I fill heaven and earth?" declares the LORD.
JEREMIAH 23:24

Evil lurks in shrouded places, the murky crevices of life. It hates the light. So sin tries to conceal itself.

We might think we're hiding our secret little sins from God, but there is no such thing as secrets from God. He sees all. And to believe that some sins are small is a lie we create to make ourselves feel better. Hiding from God? It is the dream that we wouldn't want to come true.

Still, though, we try to live in the shadows. Fearful of stepping into the light of heaven—His light. Because once bathed in His divine illumination, we can never see sin the same way again. As something livable. Doable. Acceptable. In that light we see that we are naked just as Adam and Eve did after their disobedience. We see what must be changed. Our hearts. Our minds. All of our being. In that holy light we see love in a new way. We long for goodness. We desire to be clothed in righteousness. We can see our way to heaven.

Let us step out of the dark corners of sin and into the light of Christ, where we can confess our sins and accept His love and forgiveness. Where eternal life will be ours.

Savior God, give me the strength to step into Your holy,
cleansing light. Amen.—AH

Praying the Scriptures

*All Scripture is God-breathed and is useful for teaching,
rebuking, correcting and training in righteousness.*
2 TIMOTHY 3:16

Have you ever needed a little help with your prayers? You wanted to say more that was on your heart, but you couldn't quite put it into words? Since the entire Bible is God breathed, and it is valuable in many ways, using the scriptures to help you pray is a wonderful way to speak the truth and get right to the heart of what you're trying to say.

Here's an example from Psalm 103:1–5. In this passage, the second-person reference has simply been changed to first person. But to repeat the Psalms or any other scripture in this way is not to be thought of or used as a chant as some people do in other religions. Nor are we to think that there is supernatural power in the words themselves, for it is God who is all-powerful and who hears and responds to our petitions.

Try infusing your prayers with a helping from God's holy Word.

Praise the LORD, my soul; all my inmost being, praise his holy name. Praise the LORD, my soul, and forget not all his benefits— who forgives all my sins and heals all my diseases, who redeems my life from the pit and crowns me with love and compassion, who satisfies my desires with good things so that my youth is renewed like the eagle's.

*Lord, infuse my prayers with passion, sincerity, and praise.
May our communion be beautiful and strong. Amen.*—AH

Expect a Miracle

You turned my wailing into dancing;
you removed my sackcloth and clothed me with joy.
PSALM 30:11

How do you rise up from your prayer time with the Lord? Be honest. As if nothing will really happen? As if your words have flowed from your heart and will spill into nothingness? Or perhaps you go away from your prayers with enthusiasm and heartfelt faith, but by the afternoon you are weary and disheartened again. In a world that doesn't believe in the supernatural, it is easy to make assumptions that a miracle is impossible. That miracles only happened in biblical times. Or the assumption that miracles seem to be for everyone—but you.

And yet that is not the truth.

God does hear our prayers. He does listen. He will respond. He already knows our every need. Know that in His timing our tears will turn to joy. That our hobbling, stumbling, pain-filled steps will turn to dancing. It will be in His way, His timing. Don't struggle in this truth, but rest in its beauty. The Lord's timing is perfect, and His answers are full of mercy and justice and love.

Pray.

Expect a miracle.

Keep the faith.

Sovereign God, forgive my unbelief and give me great faith. Help me to trust in Your plans and remember that in all things, You work for the good of those who love You. Amen.—AH

Spa Day for the Soul

*One of those days Jesus went out to a mountainside to pray,
and spent the night praying to God.*
LUKE 6:12

We women enjoy going to the spa—relaxing with a hot stone massage or getting our toenails painted the color of red-hot candies. Or indulging in a facial that sends us into orbital bliss. Gotta love it, eh?

We like to spoil our bodies in every way. But what about pampering our spirits? We tend to neglect what can't be seen, and yet we are made of spirit as well as flesh. So, what about having a spa day for the soul? Talk about rejuvenating. We would come away with a new outlook, a smile on our lips, and a song in our hearts. Our spirits might even feel ten years younger.

When Jesus walked among us, He showed us how important prayer was. It says in God's Word that Christ went out to the mountainside to pray and spent the night praying to God. He knew how powerful and vital prayer was and how He needed it to stay the course.

So, are you ready to schedule a spa day for your soul? A day of prayer and communion with your Lord? Or even an hour on Sunday? The luxury of this refreshment is gratis, and its beautification will be a lift to the body and spirit.

*Lord, help me to remember to regularly refresh my spirit through prayer.
My soul needs You as much as my body needs oxygen. Amen.—AH*

Way Off Balance

"I have come that they may have life, and have it to the full."
JOHN 10:10

We've all heard the racket that a washing machine can make when it goes off balance in the spin cycle. It's a *kabang, kabang, kabang* that will either drive you nuts or make you sprint into the laundry room to shift the contents around in hopes of a smoother ride for your clothes—and for your brain. Don't some days or even whole weeks seem to have that same off-balanced *kabang*? You know what I mean? People say ugly things. Your family and friends misunderstand you even though you meant well. Your boss treats you a little lower than the dust. Your body seems to be falling apart. You find yourself in a heap of trouble, and you have no idea how to make things right.

We desperately want to sprint into some celestial laundry room to fix the load. To put everything back in balance, so our lives—as well as our pounding heads—will stop with that infernal kabanging. Yet we can do nothing on our own.

God made the universe, and so He is the only One who can fix this sin-riddled, off-balanced planet of ours.

When Jesus came to earth, He willingly gave up His life as atonement for our sins. Jesus is the world's stability, and that beautiful balance, that full life, that quiet rest, is only a prayer away.

Jesus, please give me the stability and peace that can only come from You. I place my life in Your hands. Amen.—AH

The Hardest Prayer

Going a little farther, he fell with his face to the ground and prayed,
"My Father, if it is possible, may this cup be taken from me.
Yet not as I will, but as you will."
MATTHEW 26:39

When we pray, asking God for help, we have a good idea of what we want. We might even think, *This is my life. I'm the one living it, and I know exactly what I need.*

Yet we don't. We can't possibly know. We are human and more than a little fallible. Only God knows exactly what we need. So, when we pray, we should end our petitions with, "Your will be done." Hmmm. We've got to put a bit of thought into that part of the prayer. It means we'd have to trust God for our every need. All the time. Night and day. Uh-oh. Do we really trust Him that much?

Even Jesus, on the night before His crucifixion, when He knew He would be betrayed by His followers and die a brutal death on the cross, still ended his prayer with—"Your will be done." Yes, Jesus did ask God for a way out—in other words, was there another way for redemption to come to man other than His death on the cross? In fact, Christ asked God this question three times. But in the end, our Lord said the words, "Your will be done."

Jesus trusted. And so should we.

God, even when I am discouraged and afraid, help me to trust in Your will for my life. You know what's best. Amen.—AH

No Other Name

For this reason I kneel before the Father, from whom every family in heaven and on earth derives its name.

Ephesians 3:14–15

Some family names are problematic. Perhaps they resemble the people they represent a little too closely (the Stouts, who are just a wee bit on the heavy side), or perhaps the name doesn't seem to fit at all (the Loves, who are not loving at all). Or perhaps the family name is fine alone, but then becomes a problem when joined with another (Mrs. Mary Stout-Bottom might want to rethink that hyphen).

Here in his letter to the Ephesians Paul is referring to the fact that every family (in Greek, *patria*) comes from the Father (in Greek, *pater*). We are one, down to our roots, even our root word. As Paul goes on to describe, we are "rooted and established in love" (v. 17). So whether the knee that kneels before the Father is Gentile or Jew; black, white, or brown, or some color in between; clothed in rich silk or showing through shredded denim—no matter where your family line has now ended up or what convoluted path it took to get here, no matter what, you can now come freely before the God in heaven and call Him Father.

And maybe in prayer, every family can set aside prejudices and fears and for a moment grasp "how wide and long and high and deep is the love of Christ" (v. 18).

Father God, teach me how to love like You. Amen.—ML

Meet, Pray, Love

*Dear children, let us not love with words or speech
but with actions and in truth.*
1 JOHN 3:18

This verse is often used to lecture Christians today who are happy to sit in pews on chairs and listen to sermons about love and generosity, yet go out into the streets and refuse to give a homeless man a hand. It is true. You cannot just pray for people and then, when faced with a real, live, breathing person in front of your face, refuse to do him some good. You must act, for as James famously penned, "faith by itself, if it is not accompanied by action, is dead" (2:17).

Sometimes it is also true that that action involves words and speech. You can love someone through prayer. At times the most loving thing you can do for a person is pray with her and for her. When a person is deep in grief, holding her hand and praying with her for comfort is worth a whole shop full of flowers. When a person is stuck in depression, seeking him out and thanking God for him can be better than any other act. When a person is anxious, a walk out in the fresh air with a friend and a request to God for calm and assurance can be just exactly what the doctor ordered.

Love with actions. But love with words and speech, too. And do all of it in truth.

Dear God, help me to have courage to pray with others. Amen.—ML

Tongue Twister

Now you must also rid yourselves of all such things as these:
anger, rage, malice, slander, and filthy language from your lips.
COLOSSIANS 3:8

Perhaps there are people who can pray with profanity, but that would be a peculiar possibility. It would be akin to sending stinky bouquets or mailing love letters laced with lies.

No, going to God is likely to have the same effect on a person's tongue as sitting in a pew with a priest or realizing a child is in earshot. We all try to put on our Sunday-best speech when praying.

So, if you happen to be a person who has some trouble controlling your tongue, you might try this exercise: every time you want to swear, or spew angry insults, or call someone names, pray instead. Pray for self-control. Pray for patience. Pray for kindness. Pray for courtesy. Pray for respect. Pray for a better heart. Pray for more grace. Pray for the people you are angry with. Pray for the project that is causing you to curse. Pray for the coworker who gets on your last nerve. Pray for the ones who have hurt you. Pray for God's vengeance and not your own.

Pray for a new vocabulary.

Dear Lord, please make me tongue-tied
at just the right times. Amen.—ML

Confidence

*Let us then approach God's throne of grace with confidence,
so that we may receive mercy and find grace to help us in our time of need.*
HEBREWS 4:16

Do you have a robe-and-slippers friend? Someone who could just show up at your door on a Saturday morning, and you'd be in your robe and slippers, and she wouldn't care? It's a wonderful thing to have a friend so close, you know you could approach her at any time of day, in any state, and no matter what, she'd make time for you.

It is an even more wonderful thing to know that our God, the King of kings and Lord of lords, allows us—invites us—to approach His throne with confidence. He tells us to have confidence for two reasons. The first is that He understands. He has experienced everything we have, and more. He knows what it is like to be us—he has felt the weakness of the human form and the vulnerability of the human heart. The second reason is that He overcomes. He has experienced all this, and yet not succumbed to the sinful will. He was obedient, even to death.

So this is our God. He understands and overcomes and lives today. He invites us to come to Him, fully trusting that He will accept us as we are.

Even in our robe and slippers.

---

*Lord God, I bow in awe of Your grace and mercy.
Let me learn how to live for You. Amen.*—ML

An Offering

May my prayer be set before you like incense;
may the lifting up of my hands be like the evening sacrifice.
PSALM 141:2

It is not entirely clear exactly why or when the custom of burning incense as a part of religious practices came to be. Perhaps it was a way to mask the odor of the dead animals killed and burned as sacrifices to God. Perhaps it was a way to both literally and figuratively clear the air between the people and God. Or perhaps it was just that people like nice-smelling things.

For whatever reason, the burning of incense continues to this day to be an important part of many religious services. It is an expression of something from us going up to heaven. An aromatic love letter to God.

The offerings of old given to God had to be pure, clean, and whole. So we should try to come before God either in that form, or ready to submit to Him making us so.

"May my prayer be set before you like incense"—strong and sweet words, full of life. "May the lifting up of my hands be like the evening sacrifice"—empty of self and wholly devoted to the will of the Lord.

Lord, make me a living sacrifice. Amen.—ML

Call to Me

*"Call to me and I will answer you
and tell you great and unsearchable things you do not know."*
JEREMIAH 33:3

The word *unsearchable* seems a near impossibility in today's technological age. Is there anything that Google cannot search for? Apparently so.

God tells us to call to Him and He will answer. That arrangement alone is a miracle in itself—that the Lord of the universe would even want us to speak to Him. But even more amazing is the idea that God would let us in on His secrets—that He would take the time and effort to be our teacher.

This relationship with God, this closeness, is reflected again and again in scripture. It's there in Abraham staring at the stars, it's there in Moses on the mountain, and it's there in Mary's womb. God wants us to know, to be certain of the fact that He is with us, in us, through us.

God wants more from us than a Q and A session. He wants a constant conversation. He wants more than what we might "ask Siri." He wants to know the deepest questions of our souls—the ones that keep us up at night, or frighten us with their proportions.

Oswald Chambers says in *My Utmost for His Highest*, "We look upon prayer as a means of getting things for ourselves; the Bible's idea of prayer is that we may get to know God Himself."

Dear Lord, thank You for the chance to know You more. Amen.—ML

Anything

"You may ask me for anything in my name, and I will do it."
JOHN 14:14

Anything. Ask anything. That's what Jesus said. And Jesus doesn't lie.

Humans are funny creatures. God gave us the gift of speech and we just can't seem to stop getting tripped up on words. The God who knows every tongue is not so concerned with words—His concern is meanings.

So Jesus says, "Ask anything," and visions of cars, houses, and perfect hair pop into our heads. But the sentences before and after help us to understand the meaning. "I will do whatever you ask in my name, so that the Father may be glorified in the Son" (v. 13). The point of the *whatever* here is that it needs to be something that would bring glory to God. How do you do that? Read the next verse: "If you love me, keep my commands." By being obedient to Jesus, we will do what is needed to love God and love others—bringing glory to God in the process (and not to ourselves).

If we are busy keeping Jesus' commands and thinking about glorifying God, there's a good chance we won't ask for just "anything." We'll ask for what we need to fulfill those commands. We'll ask for what we need to glorify God. Peace. Faith. Grace. Mercy. Love. Courage. We'll ask for the things that count.

Anything.

Dear Father, help me know what to ask for. Amen.—ML

With Authority

"Therefore I tell you, whatever you ask for in prayer, believe that you have received it, and it will be yours."
MARK 11:24

The scene in Mark 11 brings to mind any stereotypical mob boss out for a stroll. If the big guy doesn't get what he wants, he just "takes care" of things. Ba-da-bing, ba-da-boom, no more problems.

Jesus was hungry. And apparently, a little grumpy. He spies a fig tree with leaves on it—but no figs. What gives? (Never mind that it wasn't fig season. A good tree bears fruit, right?) So Jesus curses the tree.

His fellas hear all this, but no one's gonna be a tree hugger. They continue on their way to Jerusalem, where Jesus goes into one of the most glorious rages ever described in the Bible. (Told you He was grumpy.) He literally puts the fear of God into the rival gang (the chief priests and teachers of the law).

The guys are walking back home from all this excitement when they come upon a black, gnarled stump of a tree—the fig tree, withered right down to its roots. Jesus tells them that if they believe what they say will happen in prayer, it will be done.

Who could have questioned Him? No one. And that's the point of Mark 11.

Jesus was not just another teacher or nice guy. Jesus was God. When God says your prayers will make things happen, you'd better believe Him.

God, help me make things happen for Your kingdom. Amen.—ML

Lady Persistence

"Will not God bring about justice for his chosen ones,
who cry out to him day and night?"
LUKE 18:7

Sometimes—admit it—you feel like giving up. You have a chronic illness that just never seems to get any better. You have a workload that never lets up. You have some family struggle that just cannot be resolved, no matter how hard you try.

Keep praying.

You keep trying to learn a new thing, but your grades don't show your effort. You want a relationship to work, but you don't know what to do. You keep looking for a job, but no one seems to be hiring.

Keep praying.

Jesus painted the picture for us of a widow bringing a complaint before a judge. She wanted justice. The uncaring judge wanted to be left alone. But the widow kept coming, no matter how many times he refused her. Finally, he gave in, and actually did the right thing.

Jesus pointed out that if unjust judges here on earth can decide cases to bring about justice, then God certainly can and will do the same for His children. He won't keep putting them off. He will always see that justice gets done.

Dear Judge of all, please help bring justice and peace
to the situation on my mind. Amen.—ML

Refresh

*"Repent, then, and turn to God, so that your sins may be wiped out,
that times of refreshing may come from the Lord."*
ACTS 3:19

Surely one of the prayers most often prayed is "God, I'm sorry." It must be right up there with "God, help!"

Prayer is a profound and essential part of repentance. You cannot repent without coming before God. In our present time, you cannot come before God without prayer.

Certainly it's not anyone's favorite prayer to say. To come before the Holy One and declare the ways in which you have been most definitely not holy is uncomfortable, to say the least. For some the encounter could even be sickening.

You cannot get rid of a wound without exposing it and cleaning it out. You cannot repent and start to heal without exposing your heart to God.

Let God wipe away your sins. Let God forgive you, so you can know how to forgive others. Start over. Start fresh.

Then don't take the same steps when you walk away. Try something new. Walk a different way. Set up a new routine. Make sure prayer is part of your daily schedule. Not just one part. Let prayer prepare you for your day, let prayer be a time of rest throughout your day, and let prayer end your day with thanksgiving. If you do this, the times of refreshing will come.

Dear Lord, refresh my spirit and renew my heart. Amen.—ML

Like an Eagle

*Like an eagle that stirs up its nest
and hovers over its young. . . The LORD alone led him.*
DEUTERONOMY 32:11–12

It is good to remember the kind of person we are addressing when we pray. God is mighty like the ocean, and strong like the wind. God is unending like the sky and enduring like the mountains. God is peaceful like a quiet sea and patient like shore rocks that take the waves. God is all-powerful, all-knowing, always with us.

God is big and unsearchable in many ways. Yet He lets us know Him and learn about Him. God is a whispering voice in our souls and yet His Word shouts truth.

God is huge and grand and impossible to fathom. He is our Father—Deliverer of justice, Ruler of peace, Rescuer and Redeemer.

God is like the eagle, which nurtures its eggs, turning them over at just the right time and keeping them at just the right temperature for proper growth. God is like the eagle, which protects its young chicks, covering them with its wings. God is like the eagle, playing with its young, letting them take chances and then always being there to catch them when they fall.

God is like the eagle, teaching us to fly and carrying us high over the hard parts.

This is the God we call on when we pray.

Dear God, thank You for Your tender, caring love. Amen.—ML

Near

What other nation is so great as to have their gods near them the way the LORD our God is near us whenever we pray to him?

Moses makes a rather undeniable point in his speech to the Israelites. He reminds them what God has done for them and the way in which God has spoken to them. He reminds them of these things as a warning to them not to try to make a form to fit God—not to worship idols of their own making.

Look around at the people who were living at the time and it's not hard to see why this warning was needed. Many people worshipped other gods, often linked with the seasons or natural elements. For every god they had, they had a form. It was common for people to create shapes and pictures and statues to represent their gods. People like to have something to hold on to—a way of understanding something that they can't understand.

Moses reminds the people that they need not do that. They don't have to paint a picture or shape a statue. God is right there with them. They can know Him by His voice, by His commands He has given them, and by the promises He made to them. They can be sure of Him by remembering all He has done for them, and telling these stories to the next generation, so they remember, too.

God is near. No other god comes close.

Dear God, thank You for coming near. Amen.—ML

Waiting for Mercy

But you, dear friends, by. . .praying in the Holy Spirit,
keep yourselves in God's love as you wait for the mercy of our
Lord Jesus Christ to bring you to eternal life.
JUDE 1:20–21

Some people actively long for heaven. For various reasons, they are finished with this world and ready to move on to the next.

Jude reminds you that you must keep growing in the knowledge and love of God, even when you are done with the ways of this world. You must keep "building yourselves up in your most holy faith" (v. 20). You must keep reading God's Word, studying its meaning, and living a life of service and obedience and hope.

You must keep "praying in the Holy Spirit." You must regularly go to God in prayer, spending time listening to what He has for you and time laying your requests before Him. You must let God search your mind and heart and discover any wrong thinking or wrongdoing in you. You must continue to ask forgiveness for your sins.

By doing these things, you will keep "in God's love as you wait for the mercy of our Lord Jesus Christ to bring you to eternal life."

You may be done with this world, but God is not done with you. Wait for God's mercy, but don't wait in idleness. Wait and hope and pray.

Dear Lord Jesus, we long to live with You.
Please come soon. Amen.—ML

A Prayer for Pastors

Pray also for me, that whenever I speak, words may be given me so that
I will fearlessly make known the mystery of the gospel.
EPHESIANS 6:19

How often do you pray for pastors? Pastors may be paid or not, but they are people who devote the majority of their lives to the teaching, development, care, counseling, and nurturing of God's flock. They serve in one of the hardest and most stressful jobs a person can have. Why? Because their job 100 percent of the time is dealing with people— and most often people in some kind of physical, spiritual, mental, or emotional need.

So pray for your pastors. Pray that they be able to endure long nights and long phone calls. Pray that they have time to study and be refreshed. Pray that they have clear understanding of God's Word and ability to speak truth well.

Pray for courage. Pray that they will not be afraid to stop someone from a life of destruction. Pray that they will be confident in God's love for them. Pray they will be strong in fighting off temptation.

Pray for wisdom. Pray that they will be able to pick their battles. Pray that they will know when to be silent. Pray that their understanding of people will be strengthened by experience and by prayer.

Pray for an unending well of energy. Pray for the ability to share unconditional love. Pray for an eternal life with God.

Pray for your pastors.

Dear God, thank You for Your servants.
Please help me to build them up. Amen.—ML

Inner Thoughts

For who knows a person's thoughts except their own spirit within them?
1 CORINTHIANS 2:11

Where do your thoughts roam in the space of one day?

From wondering what to cook for supper, to thinking about your own queasy stomach, to dwelling on what disease you might have, to getting distracted with that cute video of the singing kitten, to remembering the dog needs its shots, to wishing you didn't have so many things on your to-do list, to being frustrated over the state of your house, to being frustrated over the state of your country, to listening to the news, to listening to your friend and wondering why she gets herself in such messes, to wondering about your own messes—the list could go on and on, couldn't it?

That's just one normal day. Or maybe ten minutes.

No matter how close you are to someone, it's impossible to know another person's thoughts all the time. Yet the spirit within us knows. And the Spirit of God knows the thoughts of God. So with that Spirit given to us by God, when we pray and ask, we can know, a little, about what God wants for us. That Spirit prays for us when we have no words, laying our thoughts before God. It's frightening and wonderful all at the same time.

Kind of like your thoughts.

Dear God, help me to guard my thoughts from evil. Amen.—ML

All Day Long

Guide me in your truth and teach me,
for you are God my Savior, and my hope is in you all day long.
PSALM 25:5

There was once a popular candy that people called an all-day sucker. The reason it had this name, of course, is that it was such a big lollipop, it was supposed to last through a kid's licks all day long.

Let's face it. That's a lot to ask of a sucker. Most kids are content to lick a little, but at some point the urge to crunch and consume that candy conquers all. *Crunch, crunch*—and it's gone. It would be surprising if it lasted past lunchtime, much less all day.

Sometimes our focus on God doesn't make it that long, either. But it is such a relief to know that God is infinitely more durable than an all-day sucker, and He is always available to us. Whether we take a day and just reflect on Him the entire day, or whether our thoughts flit back and forth between earthly concerns and more spiritual matters, God is always ready to listen to us.

There is no time when it is not appropriate to call on Him. Unlike the all-day sucker, which might get frowned upon at formal gatherings, God's truth is always applicable. Every occasion can be a time to learn something about and lean on God. All we have to do is ask, and He will guide us.

Dear God, I place my hope in You. Amen.—ML

Son Though He Was

*He offered up prayers and petitions with fervent cries and tears
to the one who could save him from death.*
HEBREWS 5:7

There's an amazing description of Jesus in Hebrews 5. It's not long, and it's not poetically written (like the oft-quoted passages in Isaiah). It's striking in the depiction of our Savior as our brother.

Jesus walked on this earth with us. He was born and died, like we are born and will die. He suffered more than we could ever know. Just as there come days when we lift up desperate prayers to God through tears, Jesus prayed and cried, too. Just as we sometimes have to face hard things and are not given an easy out, Jesus didn't get the easy way out, either. He prayed and asked, "God please, if. . ." But He did not get the "if." He got the "Thy will be done" part instead.

Son though He was, His burdens were not taken away.

Son though He was, He was not rescued in a daring last-minute escape.

Son though He was, He did not triumph over His captors. At least, not that time.

Instead, Son though He was, He "learned obedience from what he suffered" and, then when he had fulfilled the prophecies and conquered death, he "became the source of eternal salvation for all who obey Him" (vv. 8, 9).

Why should we expect answers to our prayers to be different from His—Son that He is?

Dear God, help me to accept Your will. Amen.—ML

Prayer of a Righteous Person

Therefore confess your sins to each other and pray
for each other so that you may be healed.
JAMES 5:16

James is a clear, practical writer. In chapter 5 of his message, James tells the hearers when to pray. "Is anyone among you in trouble?" Pray. "Is anyone happy?" Praise God. "Is anyone among you sick?" Gather your church elders and let them pray over you (vv. 13, 14).

He gives you the results with complete confidence as well. "And the prayer offered in faith will make the sick person well; the Lord will raise them up. If they have sinned, they will be forgiven" (v. 15). He urges people to pray for each other so they can receive healing, for "the prayer of a righteous person is powerful and effective" (v. 16).

Why is the prayer of righteous people so powerful and effective? There are at least three reasons: 1) the faith they have; 2) the faith people have in them; 3) the faith they don't have yet. A righteous person is a faithful person—a person who knows God, and whose hope is consistently settled on God. When she prays, God knows she means it. The people who hear her know it, too. They see the righteous person's life and who her hope is in, and this strengthens their faith.

Lastly, the prayer of the righteous is powerful because of what they lack. God's strength shines in their weakness.

Dear Lord, thank You for righteous people who trust in You. Amen.—ML

Friend and Intercessor

*"My intercessor is my friend
as my eyes pour out tears to God."*
Job 16:20

Job was a man in need of a true friend. You have probably heard about the suffering of Job. (If you haven't, read the first couple of chapters of the book of Job—but be prepared for a shock.) The story of Job is about a man full of grief and hurt, a man allowed by God to be tested. He was surrounded by so-called friends, who perhaps meant well, but whose words weren't exactly helpful. About them Job said, "You are miserable comforters, all of you!" (v. 2), and he was right.

We have a better friend and comforter than any person we could find on earth. We have Jesus. Jesus is always there for us. Jesus speaks to God on our behalf. Can we imagine a better person to stand up for us? Jesus "pleads with God as one pleads for a friend" (v. 21).

And what does He plead? When we repent of our sins, He pleads for our forgiveness. When we have been hurt, He pleads for our restoration. When we stand before God to be judged for our worth, He stands in for us and says, "I make this one worthy."

It is good to have friends in high places. It's better still to have a friend willing to bring us up with Him.

Dear Jesus, thank You for pleading for me. Amen.—ML